Gesture Recognition

Gesture Recognition
Theory and Applications

QIGUANG MIAO
The School of Computer Science and Technology,
Xidian University, Xi'an, P.R. China

YUNAN LI
The School of Computer Science and Technology,
Xidian University, Xi'an, P.R. China

XIANGZENG LIU
The School of Computer Science and Technology,
Xidian University, Xi'an, P.R. China

RUYI LIU
The School of Computer Science and Technology,
Xidian University, Xi'an, P.R. China

ELSEVIER

Elsevier
Radarweg 29, PO Box 211, 1000 AE Amsterdam, Netherlands
125 London Wall, London EC2Y 5AS, United Kingdom
50 Hampshire Street, 5th Floor, Cambridge, MA 02139, United States

MATLAB® is a trademark of The MathWorks, Inc. and is used with permission. The MathWorks does not warrant the accuracy of the text or exercises in this book. This book's use or discussion of MATLAB® software or related products does not constitute endorsement or sponsorship by The MathWorks of a particular pedagogical approach or particular use of the MATLAB® software.

Notices
Knowledge and best practice in this field are constantly changing. As new research and experience broaden our understanding, changes in research methods, professional practices, or medical treatment may become necessary.

Practitioners and researchers must always rely on their own experience and knowledge in evaluating and using any information, methods, compounds, or experiments described herein. In using such information or methods they should be mindful of their own safety and the safety of others, including parties for whom they have a professional responsibility.

To the fullest extent of the law, neither the Publisher nor the authors, contributors, or editors, assume any liability for any injury and/or damage to persons or property as a matter of products liability, negligence or otherwise, or from any use or operation of any methods, products, instructions, or ideas contained in the material herein.

ISBN: 978-0-443-28959-0

For Information on all Elsevier publications
visit our website at https://www.elsevier.com/books-and-journals

Publisher: Stacy Masucci
Acquisitions Editor: Glyn Jones
Editorial Project Manager: Naomi Robertson
Production Project Manager: Omer Mukthar
Cover Designer: Miles Hitchen

Typeset by MPS Limited, Chennai, India

Working together
to grow libraries in
developing countries

www.elsevier.com • www.bookaid.org

Contents

CHAPTER 1

Basic concepts and development of gesture recognition

1.1 Principles of gesture recognition

1.1.1 Gesture in human society

Gestures refer to silent, nonverbal communication conveying specific information through visual human actions. They can express a variety of different emotions through the movement of the hands and their coordination with the face and other parts of the body. Gestures can be either used independently like sign language or together with human language to jointly express relevant communication information [1].

As a form of communication that exists independently of language, gestures have been widely used since the origin of humans and even among advanced primates such as chimpanzees [2]. In the early stages, gestures might have conveyed very limited content. With the evolution of humanity, the expressive ability of gesture has also developed, gradually forming methods of expression containing more intricate syntax. Some studies have even demonstrated that language may have originated from forms of body language, such as gestures and hand shapes [2].

Nowadays, gestures consistently serve as an independent means of communication for deaf people. Sign language is a form of language expression characterized by systematic and conventionalized movements of the hands, face, and body. It conveys precise semantics and comprises a complete linguistic process. The process of sign language production shares a neural basis similar to that of spoken language. As stated by Fu et al. [3], sign language is a communication tool designed for all deaf people. It is directly related to people's expressive activities and has evolved through long-term social practice. Deaf people's sign language is closely linked to their thoughts, featuring its own set of fundamental vocabulary and specific grammatical rules. While natural language relies on vocabulary and grammar, sign language replaces these components with various hand movements. Some sign language researchers even represent the fundamental hand shape movements of sign language as "morphemes" and use arrows to indicate the direction

Gesture Recognition
DOI: https://doi.org/10.1016/B978-0-443-28959-0.00004-2
1

of the gesture. This approach allows them to create a written representation of sign language movements, facilitating sign language instruction. It is similar to movable type, a technology in printing and typography that employs movable components. This method enables the easy and repetitive combination of basic sign language movements to form words and even complete sentences, eliminating the need for the cumbersome process of taking photos or creating drawings to record sentence content. However, with the development of various sign languages, hundreds are now in use among deaf people. Since sign languages have not yet established a universal expression method across different countries, they are still far from achieving true practicality. In addition, gestures are often employed in some specific nonvocal occasions, such as military hand signals, scuba diving hand signals, and traffic police hand signals. The sign language used in these unique situations tends to be more concise and more flexible.

On the other hand, gestures often serve as an auxiliary to spoken language, contributing to the overall communication message [4]. As shown in Fig. 1.1, the use of gestures is ubiquitous in language communication

Figure 1.1 Application of gestures in different situations[1].

---

[1] Gesture images come from the Police Gesture Dataset; see https://github.com/zc402/ChineseTrafficPolicePose for details.

across various scenarios. People frequently employ hand movements to emphasize or supplement the meaning of their spoken words. For instance, in a classroom setting, teachers often use hand movements to underscore key points during their lectures. Graziano and Gullberg [5] conducted experiments to explore the relationship between gesture and language. Their study involved different subjects, including native-language adult participants and second-language adult learners. In the experiments, subjects were initially asked to listen to a story accompanied by pictures and then relay the story's content to their partners. The results indicated a strong connection between gesture continuity and language coherence among native-speaking adult participants. When language fluency was lower, gestures appeared with more pauses, and many of them were incomplete expressions. However, in the case of second-language adult learners, when language expression became challenging, the frequency of gesture use significantly increased. In summary, in typical human-to-human communication, the influence of gesture on language expression manifests in two ways: collaboration and supplementation. On the one hand, from a communication relevance perspective, gesture serves as a complementary means of language communication. They share similarities in terms of expressive characteristics and can accompany language to reduce linguistic ambiguity. Research by Novack et al. [6] suggested that the process of using gestures in communication can reduce the cognitive load associated with language comprehension. On the other hand, gestures can also serve as a supplement to language. Compared with language communication, which relies on vocabulary and grammar, gesture communication relies more on visual and imitative imagination, and its mode of expression is more intuitive and comprehensive. It can convey meanings that language cannot express, thereby enhancing the listener's comprehension of the speaker's intent.

In addition to their role in daily communication, gestures also play an important role in the fields of art and culture. In dance and opera, gestures are often employed to express the actors' emotional changes. For example, in the renowned Dai ethnic folk dance known as the peacock dance, dancers can simulate the posture of a peacock using finger, wrist, and arm movements, showcasing the peacock's gracefulness. In the art of Peking Opera, actors often use a variety of graceful gestures to convey a strong sense of beauty, combining them with facial expressions and body movements. Peking opera artist Xu Lanyuan once remarked that in Chinese operas, each gesture serves a specific purpose, representing the essence of art. Meanwhile, many of the gestures in operas originate from religion. For example, there are many kinds of mudra in Buddhism. The Compendium of Esoteric Buddhism Mudras contains 387 different kinds of mudra patterns, many of which are similar to the hand-shaped representation of the Dan role, the female role in Chinese operas. Therefore, Yu Liwei believes that many of the gestures for the Dan role are likely to imitate or be refined from Buddhist mudra movements [7].

It can be seen that since the origin of human beings, gestures have developed as a way of communication. As a supplement to language, gestures reflect human consciousness and facilitate communication. Over time, gestures have evolved into an independent form of communication among the deaf community, giving rise to their own vocabulary and grammatical structures. Like spoken languages, gestures also have regional differences. Furthermore, gestures have been integrated into the development of human culture and art, playing an important role in dance, opera, religion, etc.

1.1.2 Gesture and human-computer interaction

Since the end of the 20th century, with the rapid development of information technology, the use of computers in both production and daily life has steadily increased, making human-computer interaction (HCI) a prominent and evolving topic. The term was introduced by Card et al. and gained popularity through their creative work, *"Human-Computer Interaction"* [8]. HCI encompasses the processes of information exchange and communication between humans and computers in various forms. It spans research across multiple disciplines, including computer science, behavioral science, industrial design, etc. HCI has a significant and profound impact on human productivity and daily life, garnering significant attention and focus from countries around the world [9].

The development of HCI can be divided into five stages: punched tape, only keyboard entry, keyboard–mouse entry, touch screen, and contactless interaction. In the earliest stages of computing, punched cards and paper tape were used for input control. However, it is highly inconvenient. Reading a small piece of data may require over 10 m of paper tape. The introduction of programming languages facilitated HCI, but it demanded extensive specialized training for users to perform input. Subsequently, the advent of the graphic user interface brought computers into the mainstream, enabling more people to control computers easily through the keyboard and mouse. After that, touch interaction became a part of daily life, presenting itself in smart terminals in various places, such as banks and airports. In recent years, the development of virtual reality technology has brought profound changes in HCI. People are increasingly looking forward to being able to get rid of the constraints of equipment and distance. Consequently, the ability to have machines respond directly to human body actions and provide corresponding results is crucial for the development of HCI.

Gesture input has become an essential technology for achieving natural and direct HCI, leveraging human perceptual capabilities and behavioral habits. With gesture input, the interaction between people and computers is no longer dependent on other media. Users can control machines using proper predefined gestures, reducing interaction complexity and significantly enhancing the overall user experience.

The definition of gesture varies across different fields. In the realm of user experience design, a widely accepted definition of gesture is that gestures are body movements that contain some information. For example, waving goodbye is a gesture, but typing on the keyboard is not. This is because the action of waving has been given the connotation of "goodbye" and can be used for interaction in itself, while the action of tapping keyboard keys with fingers does not.

Gesture recognition has been widely used across diverse HCI settings. For example, in the field of intelligent driving [10,11], in-car devices can be directly controlled by gestures, enhancing control efficiency and reducing safety risks caused by distracted driving. For entertainment [12], many video games also rely on gesture recognition. In the context of social welfare [13,14], sign language recognition technology facilitates communication for deaf people. Besides, gesture recognition has significant applications in aviation, education, and smart homes [15−20]. Therefore, studying gesture recognition algorithms with higher performance and more robustness is of great meaning.

Currently, gesture recognition technology methods for HCI can be roughly divided into two categories: methods based on wearable devices [21−25] and methods based on computer vision [26−30]. The former relies on specialized wearable devices, such as data gloves, to capture specific finger curvature and spatial position information of the hand and arm. The latter uses computer vision-related algorithms to model gestures by capturing and processing video footage of users' hand movements. Both methods have their advantages and disadvantages. The methods based on wearable devices do well in obtaining precise hand movements, including finger and wrist joint bending angles, leading to higher recognition accuracy. However, these methods require users to wear specialized equipment, which can be expensive and less convenient for everyday use. In contrast, the methods based on computer vision only require the collection of user gestures through a camera and do not impose any additional equipment on the user, making them more convenient. With advances in hardware computing power and the optimization of recognition algorithms by researchers, the methods based on computer vision have achieved improved recognition accuracy while retaining the advantages of simplicity and ease of implementation. Consequently, they offer more advantages than methods based on wearable devices.

1.2 Development of gesture recognition algorithms

As gesture recognition technology holds significant practical significance, it has drawn substantial attention from both academia and industry. As aforementioned, gesture recognition methods for HCI can be broadly categorized into two groups: those based on wearable devices and those based on computer vision. Since this book mainly studies gesture recognition methods based on computer vision, we will focus on introducing the research results in this field. As shown in Fig. 1.2, current gesture recognition methods based on computer vision can be mainly divided into the following four categories: methods based on handicraft features, methods based on probabilistic models, methods based on bag of visual words, and methods based on neural networks.

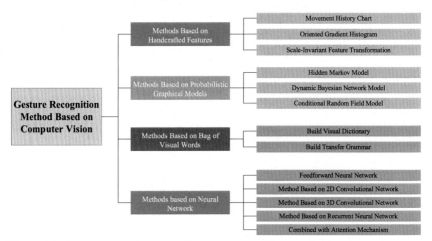

Figure 1.2 Current research status of gesture recognition methods.

1.2.1 Methods based on handicraft features

Early gesture recognition methods achieved gesture classification by extracting some handicraft features from video data and then classifying them by a support vector machine. These handicraft features are mostly designed by researchers with sufficient domain knowledge. Commonly used handicraft features include motion energy image (MEI), motion history image (MHI), histogram of oriented gradient (HOG), scale-invariant feature transform (SIFT), etc.

MEI is a binary energy graph proposed by Bobick and Davis [26]. It illustrates the trajectory of object motion and the spatial distribution of energy, and it recognizes moving objects by describing the process of the object's movement and the location of the movement in the whole space. Subsequently, they further introduced MHI. MHI is a static image accumulating changes in pixel values over a period of time at the same location, creating a static template of motion history. It aids in describing the location of motion and represents object motion through grayscale changes in the image. Compared to MEI, MHI can depict motions along with time, with the brightness value of each pixel representing the recent changes in object movement at that location. If an object's motion at a particular location is close to the current moment, the corresponding pixel's brightness in the MHI is higher. Consequently, MHI has been broadly used in the field of action recognition. Both MEI and MHI compress the temporal changes in gesture videos into a two-dimensional image, allowing for the direct study of the dynamic variations in gestures. However, the choice of parameters directly affects their ability to accurately capture complex motion changes, making these two features less suitable for describing highly intricate actions.

HOG is another common feature for describing local textures in images. This feature calculates the gradient values in different directions within local regions of an image and accumulates them. Since gradients can be higher at edges in an image, HOG describes the edges and corners of objects. Some researchers have combined HOG with optical flow to propose a new descriptor known as the histogram of optical flow (HOF) [27]. It first employs optical flow to describe motion variations and then models the gesture movements through the analysis of gradient variations of optical flow. Additionally, some researchers have explored the extension of HOG into three-dimensional space, incorporating 3D HOG features [31,32] to describe motion.

The SIFT algorithm describes features using key points such as corners and edges, which remain invariant under various affine transformations, including changes in lighting, noise, and scaling. Therefore, it is considered a robust feature and is often used in the field of gesture recognition. Based on this feature, Wan et al. [33] proposed a 3D EMoSIFT feature. This pyramid feature can detect key points of dynamic changes in the human body at different scales. It also exhibits robustness to slight movements in the background environment.

1.2.2 Methods based on probabilistic graphical model

There is a certain correlation between adjacent frames of gesture videos. Therefore, it is inappropriate to treat them as independent entities for gesture classification. Consequently, some researchers deem these frames as different variables and attempt to describe their dependencies using the probabilistic graphical model. The hidden Markov model (HMM), as well as further improved models such as dynamic Bayesian network (DBN) and conditional random field (CRF) built upon the foundation of HMM, are widely used.

Stamer and Pentl [34] employed HMM for research related to American Sign Language. Elmezain et al. [35] applied HMM to the recognition of action trajectories in dynamic gestures. Sgouropoulos et al. [36] combined neural network methods with HMM, mitigating the impact of lighting conditions on action recognition and improving recognition performance.

DBN is another general probabilistic model that can be used for both gesture recognition and localization. Du et al. [37] independently characterized the spatial positioning of objects and motion-related details using global and local features. They integrated these two types of features within a DBN framework for gesture and action recognition. Xiao et al. [38] initially extracted features from RGB and depth data, and fused these features using a DBN. Chang et al. [39] proposed a conditional dynamic Bayesian network (CDBN) to predict changes in human gestures.

In contrast to HMM, which only handles relationships between adjacent frames, CRF can address longer-term variations, making them more applicable. Wang et al. [40] added an implicit state based on CRF, called the implicit conditional random field model, and used it to identify gestures. Yulita et al. [41] utilized latent dynamic CRF to capture hidden structures within the network, enabling them to learn deeper temporal information for accurate gesture recognition.

1.2.3 Methods based on bag of visual words

The bag of words (BoW) model is a commonly used approach in the field of information retrieval. BoW does not focus on grammatical relationships within a given text but rather on establishing a dictionary for handling the set of words. The bag of visual-words (BoVW) model is a migration of the BoW model from natural language processing to computer vision. BoVW regards handicraft features such as HOG and SIFT as basic words. It selects some images from the image library to form a "visual dictionary," and formalizes the description by constructing histograms of the images. One advantage of BoVW is its modularity, i.e., the visual word bag model contains multiple submodules, each of which can be processed using different methods. By changing one of these submodules while keeping others constant, it becomes easier to assess the effectiveness of new methods.

When using the BoVW for gesture recognition, two main aspects should be taken into consideration. On the one hand, it is essential to construct an appropriate dictionary based on extracted features to cover various gesture categories. On the other hand, the grammar regarding the movement sequence of gestures should be constructed. Shen et al. [42] extracted the maximum stable extreme region features from the optical flow field. Subsequently, they applied hierarchical k-means clustering to these features to construct a visual dictionary. Finally, they used a term frequency-inverse document frequency weighting mechanism to match test gestures with data from the database, facilitating the training process. Dardas and Georganas [43] proposed a real-time gesture recognition method using the BoVW model. Their approach begins by segmenting the hand region using skin color segmentation. Next, they construct a gesture grammar, representing the corresponding state transition sequence, to describe the variations in gesture movements. It enabled them to learn dynamic gesture sequences effectively.

1.2.4 Methods based on neural network

In the early stages many researchers utilized shallow artificial neural networks (ANNs) to implement gesture recognition. Yang et al. [44] achieved dynamic gesture recognition using a time delay neural network approach to learn hand movement trajectories. The potential of deep learning in computer vision has attracted researchers, notably highlighted by the success of AlexNet [45] in the 2012 ImageNet Large-Scale Visual

Recognition Challenge. This deep learning-based model outperformed the second-place method (based on handicraft features) by nearly 11%, emphasizing the growing importance of convolutional neural networks (CNNs) in handling computer vision tasks. In the field of gesture recognition and action recognition, researchers have also proposed numerous CNN-based methods. These methods have significantly improved recognition accuracy to a large extent.

Nagi et al. [46] achieved real-time gesture recognition in the context of human-robot interaction using a convolutional neural network with a max-pooling layer. Karpathy et al. [47] obtained the foreground and background information of the video through a set of dual-path CNN networks and combined the information with different resolutions to recognize the action. In addition, they also proposed a large dataset called "Sports-1M" for action and gesture recognition. Simonyan and Zisserman [48] proposed a two-stream network for extracting temporal and spatial information from videos. Based on this model, Wang et al. [49] built a temporal segment network for video-level recognition. Wang et al. [50] combined rank pooling with CNN to extract sequence features from gesture videos.

As dynamic gesture recognition needs processing of both temporal and spatial information, some researchers have taken a different approach to introducing a three-dimensional convolutional layer to extract spatiotemporal features. It has yielded impressive results, with one notable model being the C3D model proposed by Tran et al. [51]. Afterward, many researchers have proposed many variant models. Carreira and Zisserman [52] proposed the I3D model by combining a two-stream network and an Inception unit structure. Qiu et al. [53] proposed a pseudo-3D model that replaces the 3D convolution with 2D convolution in the spatial and temporal domains to reduce time complexity. Tran et al. [54] also achieved 3D depthwise separable convolution by considering the relationships among channels in 3D CNN, simultaneously improving recognition accuracy while reducing the computational burden. Wang et al. [55] added a nonlocal mechanism on top of a 3D convolutional network to broaden the receptive field and capture a range of information changes. Feichtenhofer et al. [56] observed that each frame in a video scene typically contains two different types of regions: those with little or no change (such as the background areas) and those with significant dynamic changes (such as observed moving objects). They designed slow and fast channels to learn the overall scene information and the dynamic information about changes. Additionally, Li et al. also proposed some gesture recognition algorithms based on the C3D network, combined with the complementary relationship of RGB-D data [57], as well as the prominence of saliency data on human regions [58], and the prominence of optical flow data on dynamic regions [59]. These methods also achieved promising results.

As videos are inherently sequential data, recurrent neural networks (RNNs) and their variants are also widely employed in gesture recognition. Donahue et al. [29] used traditional CNN to extract the features of each frame and then utilized long short-term memory (LSTM) networks to learn temporal information. Molchanov et al. [28] combined C3D with RNN to implement video-based gesture detection and recognition. Pigou et al. [60] used LSTM to realize continuous gesture recognition. Zhang et al. [61] employed bidirectional LSTM to extract features from gesture videos.

In recent years, attention mechanisms have also been widely applied in computer vision. It can highlight the changes in hand movements. Narayana et al. [62] proposed FOANet, which extracts both overall video features and hand region features, yielding excellent results. Du et al. [63] generated a heatmap with an attention mechanism based on the human pose and used its auxiliary network to learn the movements of various parts of the human body, such as the head, shoulders, hands, torso, legs, and feet. Yan et al. [64] proposed a temporal convolution method for human body pose, which also assists in human action recognition.

1.3 Current challenges in the field of gesture recognition

Extensive research has been conducted in the field of gesture recognition in recent days. However, it is important to note that gesture recognition, especially in open scenarios, still faces several challenges, which can be summarized as follows:

First, there is a significant variation in how different people perform the same gesture. In an open scenario, due to divergent understandings and habits, people may perform differently in aspects such as variations in speed, amplitude, and level of adherence to norms. There can be substantial differences in the execution of the same gesture. This variability is analogous to regional dialects in a language and leads to a challenge to accurate gesture recognition.

Second, real-world environments are subject to variation. Most algorithms for gesture recognition are mainly developed and tested on datasets captured in the laboratory. However, in general datasets, training, and testing sets often have certain similarities in terms of environment, lighting, etc. In open HCI scenarios, variants such as lighting, camera angles, and performers' appearance can be divergent and are more likely to affect recognition results. Therefore, further research is needed to improve the generalization ability of the algorithms to ensure that they can be applied to real HCI systems.

Third, dynamic gesture analysis still presents challenges. Current gesture-based HCI systems always focus on recognizing static postures, which means recognizing the hands, elbows, and arms in a static image is enough. However, to achieve a richer interaction and better mimic the way people gesture and perform gestures in real environments, it is necessary to recognize sequences of consecutive gesture movements. This process requires the extraction of continuous dynamic recognition features, which undoubtedly adds complexity to recognition tasks. Therefore, applying gesture recognition in complex real-world HCI environments remains a challenging endeavor for the future.

1.4 Summary

This chapter mainly explores the concept and connotation of gesture recognition. It begins by analyzing the role of gestures in people's daily communication and daily life. Based on this, combined with the development process of HCI, the development prospects of gesture recognition as a way of human-computer interaction were explored. Subsequently, the current research methods for gesture recognition through different methods were analyzed. Finally, it discusses the issues and challenges in the field of gesture recognition, particularly in an open environment.

References

[1] Z. Hengchao, Cognitive characteristics of communicative gestures, Advances in Psychological Science 26 (5) (2018) 796−809 (张恒超. 交流手势的认知特征. 心理科学进展, 2018, 26(5): 796−809.) (in Chinese).

[2] A.S. Pollick, F.B.M. De Waal, Ape gestures and language evolution, Proceedings of National Academy of Sciences 104 (19) (2007) 8184−8189.

[3] F. Yiting, Introduction to Sign Language, Academia Press, Beijing, 1986 (傅逸亭. 聋人手语概论. 北京:学林出版社, 1986.) (in Chinese).

[4] S.D. Kelly, A. Özyürek, E. Maris, Two sides of the same coin: Speech and gesture mutually interact to enhance comprehension, Psychological Science 21 (2) (2010) 260−267.

[5] M. Graziano, M. Gullberg, Gesture production and speech fluency in competent speakers and language learners, in: Proceedings of Tilburg Gesture Research Meeting 2013. Tilburg University, 2013, pp. 1−4.

[6] M.A. Novack, E.L. Congdon, N. Hemani-Lopez, et al., From action to abstraction: Using the hands to learn math, Psychological Science 25 (4) (2014) 903−910.

[7] Y. LiWei, The inheritance and Buddhism fingerprints: two sources of Mei Lanfang's Peking Opera Gestures, Shanghai Theatre 12 (2017) 56−60.

[8] S.K. Card, T.P. Moran, A. Newell, The Psychology of Human-computer Interaction, CRC Press, Boca Raton, 1983.

[9] X. Meng, Basic Tutorial on Human-Computer Interaction, second ed., Tsinghua University Press, Beijing, 2010 (孟祥旭, 人机交互基础教程（第二版）. 北京: 清华大学出版社, 2010.) (in Chinese).

[10] P. Molchanov, S. Gupta, K. Kim et al., Multi-sensor system for driver's hand-gesture recognition, in: Proceedings of International Conference and Workshops on Automatic Face and Gesture Recognition (FG). IEEE, 2015, 1, pp. 1−8.

[11] U.E. Manawadu, M. Kamezaki, M. Ishikawa, et al., A hand gesture based driver-vehicle interface to control lateral and longitudinal motions of an autonomous vehicle, in: Proceedings of IEEE International Conference on Systems, Man, and Cybernetics, IEEE, 2016, pp. 001785−001790.

[12] X. Yuan, S. Dai, Y. Fang, A natural immersive closed-loop interaction method for human−robot "Rock−Paper−Scissors" game, Proceedings of Recent Trends in Intelligent Computing, Communication and Devices, Springer, Singapore, 2020, pp. 103−111.

[13] J.F. Lichtenauer, E.A. Hendriks, M.J.T. Reinders, Sign language recognition by combining statistical DTW and independent classification, IEEE Transactions on Pattern Analysis and Machine Intelligence 30 (11) (2008) 2040−2046.

[14] H.M. Cooper, E.J. Ong, N. Pugeault, et al., Sign language recognition using sub-units, Journal of Machine Learning Research 13 (2012) 2205−2231.

[15] D. Yang, J.K. Lim, Y. Choi, Early childhood education by hand gesture recognition using a smartphone based robot, Proceedings of IEEE International Symposium on Robot and Human Interactive Communication, IEEE, 2014, pp. 987−992.

[16] K.N. Trong, H. Bui, C. Pham, Recognizing hand gestures for controlling home appliances with mobile sensors, in: Proceedings of International Conference on Knowledge and Systems Engineering, IEEE, 2019, pp. 1−7.

[17] H.I. Fawaz, G. Forestier, J. Weber et al., Automatic alignment of surgical videos using kinematic data, in: Proceedings of Conference on Artificial Intelligence in Medicine in Europe, Springer, Cham, 2019, pp. 104−113.

[18] X. Lu, J. Shen, S. Perugini, et al., An immersive telepresence system using rgb-d sensors and head mounted display, Proceedings of IEEE International Symposium on Multimedia, IEEE, 2015, pp. 453−458.

[19] K. Cheng, N. Ye, R. Malekian, et al., In-air gesture interaction: real time hand posture recognition using passive RFID tags, IEEE Access 7 (2019) 94460−99447.

[20] X. Li, D. Guan, J. Zhang et al., Exploration of ideal interaction scheme on smart TV: based on user experience research of far-field speech and mid-air gesture interaction, in: Proceedings of International Conference on Human-Computer Interaction, Springer, Cham, 2019, pp. 144−162.

[21] S.S. Fels, G.E. Hinton, Glove-talk: a neural network interface between a data-glove and a speech synthesizer, IEEE Transactions on Neural Networks 4 (1) (1993) 2−8.

[22] D.J. Sturman, D. Zeltzer, A survey of glove-based input, IEEE Computer Graphics and Applications 14 (1) (1994) 30−39.

[23] D.L. Quam, Gesture recognition with a dataglove, Proceedings of IEEE Conference on Aerospace and Electronics, IEEE, 1990, pp. 755−760.

[24] Z. Lu, X. Chen, Q. Li, et al., A hand gesture recognition framework and wearable gesture-based interaction prototype for mobile devices, IEEE Transactions on Human-machine Systems 44 (2) (2014) 293−299.

[25] Y. Zhang, H.C. Tomo, Wearable, low-cost electrical impedance tomography for hand gesture recognition, in: Proceedings of Annual ACM Symposium on User Interface Software & Technology, 2015, pp. 167−173.

[26] A.F. Bobick, J.W. Davis, The recognition of human movement using temporal templates, IEEE Transactions on Pattern Analysis and Machine Intelligence 23 (3) (2001) 257−267.

[27] J. Konečný, M. Hagara, One-shot-learning gesture recognition using hog-hof features, The Journal of Machine Learning Research 15 (1) (2014) 2513−2532.

[28] P. Molchanov, X. Yang, S. Gupta, et al., Online detection and classification of dynamic hand gestures with recurrent 3D convolutional neural network, in: Proceedings of IEEE Conference on Computer Vision and Pattern Recognition, 2016, pp. 4207−4215.

[29] J. Donahue, L. Anne Hendricks, S. Guadarrama, et al., Long-term recurrent convolutional networks for visual recognition and description, in: Proceedings of IEEE Conference on Computer Vision and Pattern Recognition, 2015, pp. 2625−2634.

[30] Q. Miao, Y. Li, W. Ouyang et al., Multimodal gesture recognition based on the resc3d network, in: Proceedings of IEEE International Conference on Computer Vision Workshops, 2017, pp. 3047−3055.

[31] A. Klaser, M. Marszałek, C. Schmid, A spatio-temporal descriptor based on 3D-gradients, in: Proceedings of British Machine Vision Conference, 2008, pp. 1−10.

[32] A. Sanin, C. Sanderson, M.T. Harandi, et al., Spatio-temporal covariance descriptors for action and gesture recognition, Proceedings of IEEE Workshop on Applications of Computer Vision, IEEE, 2013, pp. 103−110.

[33] J. Wan, Q. Ruan, W. Li, et al., 3D SMoSIFT: three-dimensional sparse motion scale invariant feature transform for activity recognition from RGB-D videos, Journal of Electronic Imaging 23 (2) (2014) 023017.

[34] T. Starner, A. Pentl, Real-time American Sign Language recognition from video using hidden Markov models, in: Proceedings of International Symposium on Computer Vision, 1995, pp. 265−270.

[35] M. Elmezain, A. A1-Hamadi, B. Michaelis, Hand trajectory-based gesture spotting and recognition using HMM, in: Proceedings of IEEE International Conference on Image Processin, Cairo, 2009, pp. 3577−3580.

[36] K. Sgouropoulos, E. Stergiopoulou, N. Papamarkos, A dynamic gesture and posture recognition system, Journal of Intelligent & Robotic Systems (2013) 1−14.

[37] Y. Du, F. Chen, W. Xu, et al., Recognizing interaction activities using dynamic bayesian network, in: Proceedings of International Conference on Pattern Recognition, IEEE, 2006, 1, pp. 618−621.

[38] Q. Xiao, Y. Zhao, W. Huan, Multi-sensor data fusion for sign language recognition based on dynamic Bayesian network and convolutional neural network, Multimedia Tools and Applications 78 (11) (2019) 15335−15352.

[39] M.-C. Chang, L. Ke, H. Qi, et al., Fast online video pose estimation by dynamic bayesian modeling of mode transitions, IEEE Transactions on Cybernetics 51 (1) (2019) 2−15.

[40] S.B. Wang, A. Quattoni, L.P. Morency et al., Hidden conditional random fields for gesture recognition, in: Proceedings of IEEE Conference on Computer Vision and Pattern Recognition, IEEE, 2006, 2, pp. 1521−1527.

[41] I.N. Yulita, M.I. Fanany, A.M. Arymurthy, Gesture recognition using latent-dynamic based conditional random fields and scalar features. Journal of Physics: Conference Series 812 (1) (2017) 012113.

[42] X. Shen, G. Hua, L. Williams, et al., Dynamic hand gesture recognition: an exemplar-based approach from motion divergence fields, Image and Vision Computing 30 (3) (2012) 227−235.

[43] N.H. Dardas, N.D. Georganas, Real-time hand gesture detection and recognition using bag-of-features and support vector machine techniques, IEEE Transactions on Instrumentation and Measurement 60 (11) (2011) 3592−3607.

[44] M.H. Yang, N. Ahuja, M. Tabb, Extraction of 2D motion trajectories and its application to hand gesture recognition, IEEE Transactions on Pattern Analysis and Machine Intelligence 24 (8) (2002) 1061−1074.

[45] A. Krizhevsky, I. Sutskever, G.E. Hinton, Imagenet classification with deep convolutional neural networks, in: Proceedings on Advances in Neural Information Processing Systems, 2012, pp. 1097−1105.

[46] J. Nagi, F. Ducatelle, G.A. Di Caro et al., Max-pooling convolutional neural networks for vision-based hand gesture recognition, in: Proceedings of IEEE International Conference on Signal and Image Processing Applications. IEEE, 2011, pp. 342−347.

[47] A. Karpathy, G. Toderici, S. Shetty et al., Large-scale video classification with convolutional neural networks, in: Proceedings of IEEE Conference on Computer Vision and Pattern Recognition, 2014, pp. 1725−1732.

[48] K. Simonyan, A. Zisserman, Two-stream convolutional networks for action recognition, in: Proceedings on Advances in Neural Information Processing Systems, 2015, pp. 1−11.

[49] L. Wang, Y. Xiong, Z. Wang, et al., Temporal segment networks: towards good practices for deep action recognition, in: Proceedings of European Conference on Computer Vision. Springer, Cham, 2016, pp. 20−36.

[50] P. Wang, W. Li, S. Liu et al., Large-scale continuous gesture recognition using convolutional neural networks, in: Proceedings of International Conference on Pattern Recognition (ICPR), IEEE, 2016, pp. 13−18.

[51] D. Tran, L. Bourdev, R. Fergus et al., Learning spatiotemporal features with 3D convolutional networks, in: Proceedings of IEEE International Conference on Computer Vision, 2015, pp. 4489−4497.

[52] J. Carreira, A. Zisserman, Quo vadis, action recognition? a new model and the kinetics dataset, in: Proceedings of IEEE Conference on Computer Vision and Pattern Recognition, 2017, pp. 6299−6308.

[53] Z. Qiu, T. Yao, T. Mei, Learning spatio-temporal representation with pseudo-3D residual networks, in: Proceedings of IEEE International Conference on Computer Vision, 2017, pp. 5533−5541.

[54] D. Tran, H. Wang, L. Torresani, et al., Video classification with channel-separated convolutional networks, in: Proceedings of IEEE International Conference on Computer Vision, 2019, pp. 5552−5561.

[55] X. Wang, R. Girshick, A. Gupta, et al., Non-local neural networks, in: Proceedings of IEEE Conference on Computer Vision and Pattern Recognition, 2018, pp. 7794−7803.

[56] C. Feichtenhofer, H. Fan, J. Malik et al., Slowfast networks for video recognition, in: Proceedings of IEEE International Conference on Computer Vision, 2019, pp. 6202−6211.

[57] Y. Li, Q. Miao, K. Tian et al., Large-scale gesture recognition with a fusion of RGB-D data based on the C3D model, in: Proceedings of International Conference on Pattern Recognition, IEEE, 2016, pp. 25−30.

[58] Y. Li, Q. Miao, K. Tian, et al., Large-scale gesture recognition with a fusion of RGB-D data based on saliency theory and C3D model, IEEE Transactions on Circuits and Systems for Video Technology 28 (10) (2018) 2956–2964.

[59] Y. Li, Q. Miao, K. Tian, et al., Large-scale gesture recognition with a fusion of RGB-D data based on optical flow and the C3D model, Pattern Recognition Letters 119 (2019) 187–194.

[60] L. Pigou, M. Van Herreweghe, J. Dambre, Gesture and sign language recognition with temporal residual networks, in: Proceedings of IEEE International Conference on Computer Vision Workshops, 2017, pp. 3086–3093.

[61] L. Zhang, G. Zhu, P. Shen, et al., Learning spatiotemporal features using 3DCNN and convolutional LSTM for gesture recognition, in: Proceedings of IEEE International Conference on Computer Vision Workshops, 2017, pp. 3120–3128.

[62] P. Narayana, R. Beveridge, B.A. Draper, Gesture recognition: Focus on the hands, in: Proceedings of IEEE Conference on Computer Vision and Pattern Recognition, 2018, pp. 5235–5244.

[63] W. Du, Y. Wang, Y. Qiao, Rpan: An end-to-end recurrent pose-attention network for action recognition in videos, in: Proceedings of IEEE International Conference on Computer Vision, 2017, pp. 3725–3734.

[64] A. Yan, Y. Wang, Z. Li et al., PA3D: pose-action 3D machine for video recognition, in: Proceedings of IEEE Conference on Computer Vision and Pattern Recognition, 2019, pp. 7922–7931.

CHAPTER 2

Common datasets in the field of gesture recognition

In Chapter 1, we elaborated on the importance of gesture recognition in the future development of human–computer interaction (HCI) and reviewed the development history of gesture recognition methods. It is evident that more and more algorithms with high accuracy and robustness are making a significant impact in the field of gesture recognition. To fairly compare and evaluate the performance of these methods, it is necessary to establish a unified dataset. This ensures that various algorithms are tested under the same conditions, excluding the influence of irrelevant factors on the results. The emergence of these datasets has played a significant role in advancing the field. Researchers have already established numerous public datasets for training, testing, and performance comparison of gesture recognition algorithms.

The gesture recognition data can be divided into two types based on image and video data. As shown in Fig. 2.1, image-based gesture data mainly focuses on certain fixed hand gestures without considering the other movements of the performers during the gesture execution. In contrast, as shown in Fig. 2.6, video-based gestures require attention to the entire motion process, and the semantic information is reflected through the combined changes of the palm, wrist, and arm. Therefore, the carriers of these types of gestures are usually continuous video sequences.

This chapter introduces several common datasets for image-based and video-based gestures, including specific information such as time and presenter of the dataset, data modalities involved, categories, and information about the performers. Finally, a summary and comparison of the public datasets are provided to assist researchers in selecting suitable datasets.

2.1 Image-based gesture dataset

In the previous section, the role of public datasets for gesture recognition in the advancement of the field and the differences between image-based

Gesture Recognition
DOI: https://doi.org/10.1016/B978-0-443-28959-0.00008-X

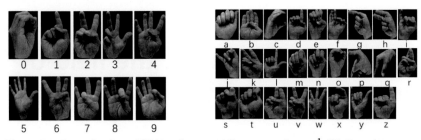

Figure 2.1 Examples from MU HandImages ASL gesture dataset[1]. (A) Complete number set with sample segmented images. (B) Complete alphabet set with sample segmented images.

and video-based data types from the perspective of data types were presented. This subsection will focus on introducing several image-based datasets, including the ASL fingerspelling dataset, the MU HandImages ASL gesture dataset, and the LaRED dataset.

2.1.1 American Sign Language fingerspelling dataset

The American Sign Language (ASL) fingerspelling recognition dataset [1], collected in 2011 by Pugeault and Bowden using the depth sensor Kinect, is a publicly available dataset. This dataset uses finger movements to represent 26 letters in written English, and fingerspelling is an essential part of ASL communication. The dataset consists of 24 different gestures performed by five gesture performers in relatively similar background conditions. These 24 gestures represent the 24 English letters from A to Z, excluding J and Z (represented by video-based gestures in frame sequences). Each gesture sample includes paired RGB and depth images. For each performer, each letter gesture contains around 500 RGB and depth images. Therefore, the total number of images in the ASL dataset amounts to about 60,000.

2.1.2 MU HandImages ASL gesture dataset

The MU HandImages ASL gesture dataset was proposed in 2011 by Barczak et al. [2] from Massey University. This dataset contains 36 gestures (including the 10 numbers from 0 to 9 and the 26 letters from A to Z) based on ASL. These gestures were performed by five performers, resulting in a total of 2,515 images. An example of this dataset is illustrated in Fig. 2.1.

---

[1] For further details, please visit http://www.massey.ac.nz/~albarcza/gesture_dataset2012.html.

This dataset has the following main characteristics:

1. A combination of lights around the camera was used to simulate different natural lighting conditions, resulting in gesture data that includes images under a wide range of illumination conditions.

2. A green screen background was provided during the shooting, and performers wore wristbands matching the background color. This allowed for the gestures to be segmented and cropped from the original image, reducing interference from the background and other irrelevant factors.

2.1.3 LaRED gesture dataset

The LaRED (large RGB-D extensible hand gesture dataset) is a large extensible hand gesture recognition dataset published in 2014 by Hsiao et al. [3]. This dataset was collected with an Intel RealSense short-range depth camera, and most of the gestures in the dataset are taken from ASL.

The LaRED dataset uses 27 gestures (labeled G001 to G027) as its basic gestures. For each basic gesture, there are three different orientations: basic gesture, basic gesture rotated 90 degrees around the x-axis, and basic gesture rotated 90 degrees around both the x-axis and y-axis, labeled as O001 to O003, respectively. The three different orientations derived from one basic gesture are considered a separate category in the dataset. Since there are 27 basic gestures, the dataset in total contains 81 gesture categories.

Each category is performed by ten performers (five males and five females), with the male performers numbered M001 to M005 and the female performers numbered F001 to F005. For each gesture category, 300 samples are collected from each performer, and each sample includes both RGB and depth images. In addition, the dataset also provides binarized mask images (i.e., image data of the hand region segmented from binarized images), totaling 243,000 images in all three categories combined.

2.1.4 Marcel gesture dataset

The Marcel gesture dataset is an image-based gesture dataset introduced by Marcel et al. [4] in 1999. It consists of six gestures (representing A, B, C, Five, Point, and V). The size of each gesture image varies in the range of 70×70 to 70×80 pixels, while the image window itself is approximately 20×20 in size. Each gesture includes both monochromatic and

Figure 2.2 Examples from Marcel gesture dataset.[2]

complex background data batches. The monochromatic background images are shown as examples in Fig. 2.2. In the literature [4], Marcel et al. use both of these two kinds of data for training and test them separately.

2.1.5 Senz3D gesture dataset

The Senz3D gesture dataset was collected in 2015 by Memo et al. researchers at the University of Padova in Italy, using the Creative Senz3D device [5,6]. This dataset includes 11 gestures presented by four performers and has 1,320 images in total. For one performer, each gesture is performed 30 times. RGB, depth, and corresponding confidence image are all available for each gesture. Compared with other datasets, images in this dataset are more realistic and have a higher resolution, reaching 640 × 480.

2.2 Video-based gesture dataset

Compared with image-based gestures, the video-based gesture is more practical since it is always required in real-world HCI scenarios. In this part, we will introduce some general video-based gesture datasets, including the 20BN-JesterdDataset, RWTH-PHOENIX-Weather, CSL series, ChaLearn series, SKIG dataset, and EgoGesture dataset.

2.2.1 20BN-jester dataset

The 20BN-Jester dataset[3] [7] is acquired by 148,092 performers from around the world, performing in front of webcams according to examples of gesture actions with simple webcams. Similar to ImageNet, the

---

[2] For further details, please visit https://www.idiap.ch/resource/gestures/.
[3] For further details, please visit https://20bn.com/datasets/jester.

representative large-scale image dataset in image recognition, the 20BN-Jester dataset is also a widely used benchmark in large-scale gesture datasets. The 20BN-Jester dataset only contains RGB modality information of gesture images. It includes 118,562 samples in the training set and 14,787 samples in both the validation and test sets. It has 27 classes of gestures, of which 26 are symmetric, such as enlarging/shrinking, scrolling up/down, etc., and the other one is a blank class, which does not involve any gesture actions.

The 20BN-Jester dataset has a large number of performers, and due to the diverse environments of the performers, there is a noticeable difference in background, lighting, and obstructions in each gesture video. The backgrounds in the video data vary, including sofas, windows, bookcases, etc., along with differences in lighting and filming angles. Additionally, the race and appearance of the performers also vary. These divergences pose significant challenges for gesture recognition.

2.2.2 RWTH-PHOENIX-weather dataset

The RWTH-PHOENIX-Weather dataset is a sign language dataset recorded by RWTH Aachen University in Germany [8,9], used for sign language interpretation of daily news and weather forecasts on the German public television channel Phoenix. The video was performed by nine different performers, comprising nearly 7,000 sentences related to weather forecasting. The dataset was recorded with an ordinary color camera, with sign language performers standing in front of a gray gradient background wearing dark-colored tops. The dataset has two versions, distinguished by the year of production as PHOENIX 2012 and PHOENIX 2014. The 2014 version is an expansion of the 2012 version. All video samples have a frame rate of 25 frames per second and a resolution of 210×260, containing only the sign language performers without other distractions. The entire dataset consists of 6,841 sentences corresponding to sign language videos, which can be divided into training, validation, and test subsets, containing 5,672, 540, and 629 videos, respectively. The RWTH-PHOENIX-Weather is one of the most commonly used sign language video datasets.

2.2.3 CSL series datasets

The Chinese Sign Language Recognition dataset[4] has been performed by Jie Huang et al. since 2015. It consists of two types of isolated sign

---

[4] For further details, please visit http://home.ustc.edu.cn/ ~ hagjie/.

language recognition (SLR) [10−13] and continuous SLR [14−16], as per the word-level or sentence-level signs. The isolated SLR includes 500 different sign language words, each with 250 samples, while the continuous SLR comprises 100 different sign language sentences, each with 50 video samples. Each video sample in the dataset is annotated by professional Chinese sign language teachers. Both datasets include three types of data modalities: RGB, depth, and skeleton data, performed by 50 performers, with each performer repeating each sign five times.

2.2.4 DEVISIGN sign language dataset

The DEVISIGN Chinese sign language dataset [17,18] funded by Microsoft Research Asia since 2012 and constructed by the Visual Information Processing and Learning Group of the Institute of Computing Technology, Chinese Academy of Sciences, provides a large-scale dataset of Chinese sign language for researchers worldwide. It offers a direction for the practical application of sign language recognition technology, especially in real-world scenarios and for massive, unlabeled, unknown user cases. The DEVISIGN dataset covers all 4,414 standard vocabularies in Chinese sign language, collected by 30 performers (13 males and 17 females), totaling 331,050 vocabulary data. Each data sample includes different modalities such as RGB, depth, and skeleton data, with RGB presented in video format. The dataset encompasses both intra- and inter-class variation of vocabularyies.

Currently, three versions of DEVISIGN-G, DEVISIGN-D, and DEVISIGN-L are released. DEVISIGN-G consists of 432 samples of the basic 26 letters and 10 numbers. DEVISIGN-D includes 6,000 samples of 500 daily vocabularies (including the 36 basic letters and numbers from DEVISIGN-G). DEVISIGN-L expands upon DEVISIGN-D, encompassing 2,000 Chinese sign language vocabularies with a total of 24,000 samples. The differences among these subsets are only in the scale of the data, with the performers and the number of collections remaining consistent to eliminate irrelevant factors affecting recognition.

2.2.5 CGD series datasets

2.2.5.1 CGD 2011

In 2011, the ChaLearn Gesture Challenge officially released the CGD 2011 gesture dataset [19]. This dataset collects gestures from nine major categories of actions, including (1) basic gestures in daily life (e.g., wearing glasses, drinking water, kicking a ball); (2) imitative actions (e.g., movements in mime performances); (3) gestures in dance; (4) unconscious movements (e.g., rubbing hands, scratching head, touching ears); (5) event-emphasizing gestures accompanying language expression (e.g., clapping to emphasize speech); (6) explanatory actions accompanying language expression; (7) ceremonial gestures (e.g., military salute, traditional Indian gestures); (8) sign language (e.g., gestures for communication in the deaf and mute community); (9) signal gestures (e.g., referee signals, diving signals, or traffic directing signals); etc.

The CGD 2011 was collected using Kinect. It includes 30 basic gestures, performed by 20 participants, totaling 50,000 gesture samples. Each frame in the video is 240×320 in size. Each gesture includes data in both RGB and depth modalities. The training set of this dataset contains 48,000 samples, and the validation set contains 2,000 samples. In addition, a test set of 4,000 samples was constructed to test the competition results. Sample illustrations are shown in Fig. 2.3, where the background and lighting conditions vary during the performers' gesture demonstrations.

2.2.5.2 CGD 2013

In 2013, the ChaLearn gesture challenge shifted its focus to multimodal gesture recognition and proposed the CGD 2013 [20] dataset. It leverages the Kinect v1 sensor for data collection and has 20 classes of Italian gestures demonstrated by 27 performers. It can be divided into training (403 samples), validation (300 samples), and test (274 samples) sets. As shown in Fig. 2.4, each sample encompasses five distinct modalities: RGB data and depth data (both at 480×640 resolution), binary mask data

Figure 2.3 Sample examples from CGD 2011 dataset.

Figure 2.4 Examples of five modal data types in the ChaLearn 2013. (A) RGB data. (B) Depth data. (C) Binary mask data. (D) Skeleton data. (E) Audio data.

Figure 2.5 CGD 2016[5] Examples of RGB sample frames and depth sample frames of gestures.

(highlights the silhouette of performers), skeleton data, and audio data with Italian interpretations corresponding to actions. Notably, the depth modality was presented as a heatmap, enhancing the dataset's utility for researchers exploring the intricate nuances of gesture recognition across multiple sensory inputs.

2.2.5.3 CGD 2016

In 2016, a new dataset (CGD 2016) [21] was proposed based on the datasets associated with the ChaLearn gesture challenge. At the time, it was the largest dataset in the field of gesture recognition. It comprises two parts: the isolated gesture dataset (IsoGD) and the continuous gesture dataset (ConGD). In IsoGD, each video contains only one gesture, whereas in ConGD, each video contains two or more gestures of different categories. As illustrated in Fig. 2.5, each sample includes data in two modalities: RGB data and depth data.

---

[5] For further details, please visit https://gesture.chalearn.org/2016-looking-at-people-cvpr-challenge/isogd-and-congd-datasets.

The IsoGD in the CGD 2016 contains a total of 47,933 gesture samples, encompassing 249 types of gestures, performed by 21 performers. This dataset is divided into three subsets: training, validation, and test sets, containing 35,878, 5,784, and 6,271 samples, respectively, performed by 17, 2, and 2 performers, with each subset of performers being distinct from the others. Notably, there is significant variation in the length of videos in this dataset, with the shortest video sequence being only nine frames and the longest being up to 405 frames.

Similar to the IsoGD, the ConGD also contains 47,933 gesture actions, totaling 22,535 video sequences. Like IsoGD, ConGD is also divided into three fixed subsets: training, validation, and test sets. However, unlike IsoGD, each video in the ConGD dataset may contain multiple gestures. This dataset requires not only the recognition of individual gesture actions but also the prediction of the sequence order, start, and end frames of each gesture. Thus, the overall recognition result of the sentence is compared with the labeled sequence samples to determine the final recognition rate, making the tasks in the ConGD more challenging than those in the IsoGD.

2.2.6 Traffic police gesture dataset

Zhang et al. [22] propose a Chinese traffic police gesture dataset[6] based on the standard traffic gestures in China. This dataset consists of 21 videos with a total of 3,354 gesture samples. The video contains multiple scenarios, including locations such as classrooms, parks, parking lots, roads, and forests. The performers have different looks and heights and must wear black clothes or traffic police clothing to cooperate with the recording. The video background objects include walls, sky, grass, roads, trees, buildings, bicycles, cars, and a small number of pedestrians who are far away. This dataset contains eight types of traffic police command gestures announced in the above notice, including straight ahead, stop, left turn, right turn, etc. [22].

2.2.7 SKIG dataset

The Sheffield Kinect Gesture (SKIG) dataset was collected and published by Liu and Shao from Sheffield University in 2013 [23]. SKIG has a total of 2,160 gesture sequences, including 1,080 RGB sequences

[6] For further details, please visit https://github.com/zc402/ChineseTrafficPolicePose.

and 1,080 depth data sequences, each of which is captured simultaneously using Kinect depth cameras.

The SKIG dataset collected ten different types of video-based gestures in six different scenarios. The classification between the ten different gestures is based on the movement trajectory of the arm. Due to the consideration of different lighting conditions, background conditions, and palm shapes during the collection of the SKIG dataset, it is suitable as experimental data for visual video-based gesture recognition research. All ten gestures were collected using three different palm shapes: clenching the fist, extending the index finger, and opening the five fingers. To increase the diversity of the same type of gesture, each gesture was collected under two types of lighting (strong and weak light) and three backgrounds (wooden board background, whiteboard background, and paper background). Therefore, in each scenario, there are 10 (categories) $\times$ 3 (palm shape) $\times$ 3 (Background) $\times$ 2 (Illumination) $\times$ 2 (Modality) = 360 gesture sequence samples. SKIG does not separate the training and testing sets. The authors suggest conducting three cross-validation partitions based on six different theme scenarios in a 2:1 ratio.

2.2.8 EgoGesture dataset

The EgoGesture dataset is a publicly available video-based gesture recognition dataset [24,25]. This dataset is a multimodal large-scale continuous gesture dataset collected from the first-person perspective for gesture recognition. A total of 83 gestures are included. Unlike most video-based datasets, such as the 20BN-Jester and ChaLearn series mentioned earlier, this dataset generally only includes changes in hand movements.

The EgoGesture dataset contains a total of 2,081 gesture videos, including 24,161 gesture samples performed by 50 different performers. A total of six scenes were designed in this dataset, including four indoor scenes and two outdoor scenes. Indoor scenes include (1) gesture videos of performers in different background environments when they are stationary; (2) gesture videos of performers in a changing background while still; (3) gesture videos of performers in the background of a window in direct sunlight while still; and (4) video of the performer's gesture while walking. Outdoor scenes include (1) video of the performer's gestures while stationary and in a changing background; and (2) video of a performer's gestures in a changing background while walking. Examples of six scenes are shown in Fig. 2.6.

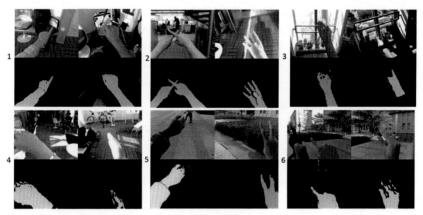

Figure 2.6 Six scenarios of EgoGesture dataset.[7]

2.2.9 MSRC-12 dataset

The MSRC-12 (Microsoft Research Cambridge-12) dataset [26] was collected and produced by Fothergill et al. from the computer laboratory of the University of Cambridge at Microsoft Research Institute in 2012 using Kinect. This dataset is composed of bone data sequences from various parts of the human body, with a total of 594 bone sequences and a total of 719,359 frame joint data. The dataset includes 12 types of gestures, performed by 30 performers. For each type of gesture, each performer will perform multiple times to form a skeletal sequence. The dataset provides the coordinates of bone data in the form of CSV files and gives the emoticons of each action (including corresponding categories and start/end frame numbers) through the tagstream file, with Matlab® code 12 attached for users to visualize bone data.

The MSRC-12 dataset contains three different types of data, namely text (textual representation of performing actions), images (an ordered set of image-based gesture performance images with appropriate annotations), and videos (continuous gesture performance videos). This dataset is collected through Kinect and consists of 20 joint points to form the skeletal information of the human body. The 12 types of actions in the dataset are divided into two categories: one is called standard action, and the action

---

[7] For further details, please visit http://www.nlpr.ia.ac.cn/iva/yfzhang/datasets/egogesture. html.

name is a direct description of the action itself. Another type of action is called metaphorical action, where the action name is associated with an implied meaning. The specific meanings of gestures in this dataset can be found in Table 2.1.

2.2.10 NvGesture dataset

The NvGesture dataset is a gesture dataset proposed by Molchanov et al. [27] in 2016 for HCI in driving. The gesture samples in this dataset are collected from different perspectives using multiple sensors, such as SoftKinetic depth cameras and stereo IRSensors, which include RGB data, depth data, and infrared data. In addition, Molchanov et al. also calculated the infrared disparity map. The frame rate of all video data is 30 frames per second, with a resolution of 320×240 per frame. In the video, the performer simulates the process of HCI while driving, holding the steering wheel with his left hand and completing the gesture with his right hand. The system prompts the performer to execute each gesture through an interface on the display screen and provides an audio description of the gesture and a five-second video sample to guide the performer to complete the demonstration of the gesture.

NvGesture dataset contains a total of 1,530 gesture video samples performed by 20 performers. The dataset is divided into two parts: a training set and a testing set, each containing 1,049 and 481 video samples. In the video, the performer simulates the process of HCI while driving, holding the steering wheel with his left hand and completing the gesture with his right hand. The dataset contains 25 types of gestures, and since this dataset is mainly used in the driving environment, the gestures in the dataset are completed only with one hand.

2.3 Dataset summary

In recent years, there has been a substantial surge in the release of datasets within the field of gesture recognition, raising interest among researchers. This section provides a comparative analysis of various gesture datasets, considering the following critical aspects.

1. More modalities of data are involved. With the development of techniques, more attention has been paid to various modalities such as RGB, depth, and infrared rather than using simple RGB input.

Table 2.1 MSRC-12 dataset gesture information.

Type	Number	Action description	Action number
Standard action	2	Crouching/hiding	G2 squat down
	4	Wear night vision goggles to change game mode	G4 Raise your hands in a grip in front of your eyes.
	6	Shoot with a pistol	G6 Extend your arms and fold your hands together to form a pistol, making a shooting gesture.
	8	Throw an object, such as a grenade	G8 Use your right arm to perform a pitch and throw motion.
	10	Change weapons	G10 The left hand naturally droops, the right hand extends behind the left shoulder, and then the hands retract back to the abdomen.
	12	Kick the enemy	G12 Kick forward with your right leg.
Metaphorical action	1	Start music/increase volume	G1 Raise your hands high and place them on both sides of your head.
	3	Switch to the next menu	G3 Place your right hand naturally on your abdomen, palm down, and then stroke from left to right.
	5	End music	G5 Circle your arms in front of you, with your right hand in a clockwise direction and your left hand in a counterclockwise direction.
	7	Bow to end the meeting	G7 Bend forward and pause for a moment before getting up.
	9	Protest music	G9 Cross your hands and place them on your head.
	11	Slow down the rhythm of the song	G11 Wave your hands on both sides of your head.

Most of the dataset mentioned above provides more than two modes of information.

2. The size of the gesture recognition dataset is also gradually increasing. Due to further exploration of this task by researchers, the types of gestures have also become more diverse. For example, the early SKIG dataset only has ten types of gestures, while the EgoGesture dataset and CGD 2016 dataset have 83 and 249 types of gesture data, respectively. The rich types of gestures provided strong support for the development of gesture recognition technology.

3. As the number of gestures in the gesture dataset increases, the application scenarios of the dataset become richer and more diverse. The EgoGesture dataset and NvGesture dataset tend to focus on gesture recognition in autonomous driving, while the RWTH-PHOENIX-Weather, CSL dataset, and DESIGN dataset are aimed at sign language learning and analysis for hearing-impaired individuals.

4. With the development of gesture recognition methods, the environment for collecting gesture recognition data is also closer to reality. A significant change is that the collection background of the dataset has become more diverse. The background of the SKIG dataset and the MU HandImages ASL gesture dataset is relatively simple, and there is no interference from the background environment. The background environment of the RWTH-PHOENIX-Weather and CGD series datasets is relatively complex, and the EgoGesture dataset and traffic police gesture dataset use different scenarios, which all enhance the challenge of gesture recognition.

Table 2.2 provides a comparison of the specific information of these datasets.

Table 2.2 mainly compares the above datasets from several aspects, such as the size of the dataset, data modality, visual angle, number of participants, and action categories. It can be seen that the current data size of the 20BN Jester dataset is much larger than other datasets, and the number of participants in the demonstration is also the highest. From the perspective of action categories, due to the large number of sign language vocabulary involved, the isolated SLR dataset is currently the largest dataset with the largest number of categories. In addition, these datasets were collected from a third-person perspective, except for EgoGesture, which was collected from a first-person perspective.

Table 2.2 Relevant information of the common benchmark dataset for gesture recognition algorithms.

Data type	Dataset		Years	Collecting device	Data modality	Category	Number of performers	Number of samples	Application
Image-based data	ASL		2011	Kinect	RGB, DEPTH	26	5	120,000	Gesture recognition
	MU HandImages ASL		2011	Kinect	RGB, DEPTH	36	5	2,515	Gesture recognition
	LaRED		2014	Kinect	RGB, DEPTH, MASK	81	10	243,000	Gesture recognition
	Marcel		1999	Ordinary camera	RGB	6	10	5,819	Gesture recognition
	Senz3D		2015	Senz3D	RGB, DEPTH	11	4	1,320	Gesture recognition
	Traffic gestures		2019	Ordinary camera	RGB	8	20	3,354	Gesture recognition
Video-based data	20BN-jester		2019	Webcam	RGB	27	1,376	148,092	Gesture recognition
	RWTH-PHOENIX-Weather		2014	Ordinary camera	RGB	400	9	45,760	Gesture recognition
	CSL	-100	2015	Kinect	RGB, DEPTH, BONES	100	50	5,000	Gesture recognition
		-500				500		125,000	
	DEVISIGN	-G	2012	Kinect	RGB, DEPTH, BONES	36	8	432	Gesture recognition
		-D				500		6,000	
		-L				2,000		24,000	
	CGD 2011		2011	Kinect	RGB, DEPTH	30	20	50,000	Gesture recognition
	CGD 2013		2013	Kinect	RGB, DEPTH, BONES, AUDIO FREQUENCY MASK	20	27	403	Gesture recognition
	CGD 2016		2016	Kinect	RGB, DEPTH	249	21	47,933	Gesture recognition
	SKIG		2013	Kinect	RGB, DEPTH	10	6	2,160	Gesture recognition
	EgoGesture		2018	RealSense	RGB, DEPTH	83	50	24,161	Gesture recognition
	MSRC-12		2012	Kinect	BONES	12	30	594	Gesture recognition
	NvGesture		2016	Kinetic, infrared camera	RGB, DEPTH, OPTICAL FLOW, INFRARED	25	20	1,530	Gesture recognition

2.4 Summary

In this chapter, we analyze existing datasets in the field of gesture recognition. We aim to provide a comprehensive overview by describing the characteristics and potential applications of available datasets and also present their inherent strengths and weaknesses. Furthermore, we study the categorization of these datasets based on the nature of data acquisition, differentiating between video-based and image-based datasets. Finally, we present a comparative examination of these datasets, considering their distinct features, modalities, and practical applications.

References

[1] N. Pugeault, R. Bowden, Spelling it out: Real-time ASL fingerspelling recognition, in: Proceedings of IEEE International Conference on Computer Vision Workshops, IEEE, 2011, pp. 1114—1119.

[2] A.L.C. Barczak, N.H. Reyes, M. Abastillas, et al., A new 2D static hand gesture colour image dataset for ASL gestures, Research Letters in the Information and Mathematical Sciences 15 (2011) 12—20.

[3] Y.S. Hsiao, J. Sanchez-Riera, T. Lim, et al., LaRED: a large RGB-D extensible hand gesture dataset, in: Proceedings of 5th ACM Multimedia Systems Conference, 2014, pp. 53—58.

[4] S. Marcel, Hand posture recognition in a body-face centered space, in: Proceedings of Conference on Human Factors in Computing Systems, 1999, 302—303.

[5] A. Memo, L. Minto, P. Zanuttigh, Exploiting silhouette descriptors and synthetic data for hand gesture recognition, STAG (2015) 15—23.

[6] A. Memo, P. Zanuttigh, Head-mounted gesture controlled interface for human-computer interaction, Multimedia Tools and Applications 77 (1) (2018) 27—53.

[7] J. Materzynska, G. Berger, I. Bax et al., The Jester dataset: A large-scale video dataset of human gestures, in: Proceedings of International Conference on Computer Vision Workshops, IEEE, 2019, pp. 1—9.

[8] J. Forster, C. Schmidt, T. Hoyoux, et al., RWTH-PHOENIX-weather: a large vocabulary sign language recognition and translation corpus, in: Proceedings of Language Resources and Evaluation Conference, 2012, 9, pp. 3785—3789.

[9] O. Koller, J. Forster, H. Ney, Continuous sign language recognition: towards large vocabulary statistical recognition systems handling multiple signers, Computer Vision and Image Understanding 141 (2015) 108—125.

[10] J. Zhang, W. Zhou, C. Xie, et al., Chinese sign language recognition with adaptive HMM, in: Proceedings of IEEE International Conference on Multimedia and Expo, IEEE, 2016, pp. 1—6.

[11] J. Pu, W. Zhou, H. Li, Sign language recognition with multi-modal features, in: Proceedings of Pacific Rim Conference on Multimedia, Springer, Cham, 2016, pp. 252—261.

[12] T. Liu, W. Zhou, H. Li, Sign language recognition with long short-term memory, in: Proceedings of IEEE International Conference on Image Processing, IEEE, 2016, pp. 2871—2875.

[13] J. Pu, W. Zhou, J. Zhang, et al., Sign language recognition based on trajectory modeling with HMMs, in: Proceedings of International Conference on Multimedia Modeling. Springer, Cham, 2016, pp. 686−697.

[14] J. Pu, W. Zhou, H. Hu, et al., Boosting continuous sign language recognition via cross modality augmentation, in: Proceedings of ACM International Conference on Multimedia, 2020, pp. 1497−1505.

[15] J. Pu, W. Zhou, H. Li, Dilated convolutional network with iterative optimization for continuous sign language recognition, in: Proceedings of International Joint Conference on Artificial Intelligence, 2018, pp. 885−891.

[16] D. Guo, W. Zhou, H. Li, et al., Hierarchical lstm for sign language translation, in: Proceedings of AAAI Conference on Artificial Intelligence, 2018, pp. 6845−6852.

[17] X. Chai, H. Wang, X. Chen, The DEVISIGN large vocabulary of Chinese sign language database and baseline evaluations, Beijing: Technical Report VIPL-TR-14-SLR-001, 2014.

[18] H. Wang, X. Chai, X. Hong, et al., Isolated sign language recognition with grassmann covariance matrices, ACM Transactions on Accessible Computing 8 (4) (2016) 1−21.

[19] I. Guyon, V. Athitsos, P. Jangyodsuk, et al., The chalearn gesture dataset (CGD 2011), Machine Vision and Applications 25 (8) (2014) 1929−1951.

[20] S. Escalera, J. Gonzàlez, X. Baró, et al., Multi-modal gesture recognition challenge 2013: dataset and results, in: Proceedings of ACM International Conference on Multimodal Interaction, 2013, pp. 445−452.

[21] J. Wan, Y. Zhao, S. Zhou, et al., Chalearn looking at people rgb-d isolated and continuous datasets for gesture recognition, in: Proceedings of IEEE Conference on Computer Vision and Pattern Recognition Workshops, 2016, pp. 56−64.

[22] J. He, C. Zhang, X. He, et al., Visual recognition of traffic police gestures with convolutional pose machine and handcrafted features, Neurocomputing 390 (2020) 248−259.

[23] L. Liu, L. Shao, Learning discriminative representations from RGB-D video data, in: International Joint Conference on Artificial Intelligence, AAAI Press, 2013, pp. 1493−1500.

[24] Y. Zhang, C. Cao, J. Cheng, et al., EgoGesture: a new dataset and benchmark for egocentric hand gesture recognition, IEEE Transactions on Multimedia 20 (5) (2018) 1038−1050.

[25] C. Cao, Y. Zhang, Y. Wu, et al., Egocentric gesture recognition using recurrent 3D convolutional neural networks with spatiotemporal transformer modules, in: Proceedings of IEEE International Conference on Computer Vision, 2017, pp. 3763−3771.

[26] S. Fothergill, H. Mentis, P. Kohli, et al., Instructing people for training gestural interactive systems, in: Proceedings of the SIGCHI Conference on Human Factors in Computing Systems, 2012, pp. 1737−1746.

[27] P. Molchanov, X. Yang, S. Gupta, et al., Online detection and classification of dynamic hand gestures with recurrent 3D convolutional neural network, in: Proceedings of IEEE Conference on Computer Vision and Pattern Recognition, 2016, pp. 4207−4215.

CHAPTER 3

Gesture recognition method based on handicraft features

3.1 Hand region segmentation

The focus of gesture recognition lies in the identification of hand movements. Consequently, a common approach in a gesture recognition method is to first separate the hand, wrist, arm, and other gesture-related areas from the complex scene through hand area segmentation. Subsequently, leveraging the motion characteristics within these segmented hand regions, models are constructed to capture the hand's movements, culminating in the recognition of gestures. Generally, gesture segmentation methods can be categorized into three categories [1]: edge information-based segmentation, motion analysis-based segmentation, and segmentation based on physical characteristics such as color. This section will delineate these three approaches.

3.1.1 Edge information-based segmentation methods

3.1.1.1 Edge operator-based segmentation approach

In an image, brightness values typically differ across regions, resulting in discernible brightness differences at the edges. Leveraging this characteristic, hand regions within the image can be isolated using edge detection methods, thereby achieving segmentation of the hand area. Edge detection in images involves two key aspects. One is the suppression of image noise to preclude extraneous edges unrelated to the hand region from calculations, and the other is the accurate localization of the edge position. Edge operators are computational units used to extract edges within an image. Common edge operators include the Prewitt, Laplacian, Roberts, and Canny operators, each exhibiting different levels of noise suppression while determining edge positions. Utilizing the Canny operator helps mitigate noise interference, thereby accurately detecting edges within the image. This is primarily due to the multistage computational process encompassing filtering, enhancement, and detection employed by the Canny operator to execute edge detection tasks. However, practical hand area segmentation tasks are often more complex. Solely applying generic

Gesture Recognition
DOI: https://doi.org/10.1016/B978-0-443-28959-0.00003-0

edge detection algorithms cannot accurately extract relevant regions. It also requires the use of other information, such as skin color. As shown in Fig. 3.1, Wang Heng [2] devises a technique combining skin color information and Canny edge detection to segment the hand area in images. Based on predetermined thresholds, this approach leverages skin color information to separate human body regions like faces and hands from the image. On this basis, capitalizing on the distinct edges of human facial regions, edge detection is used to exclude facial regions from the image, and the spatial relationship between the face and hands is utilized to extract the hand region.

Additionally, Lin et al. [3] utilize skin color information to effectively separate the human body region from the image background region. After that, based on the characteristics that the human face shape is close to elliptical with almost no deformation, while the geometric shape of the human hand has greater differences and is prone to change, they design feature parameter thresholds to extract the hand region from the image.

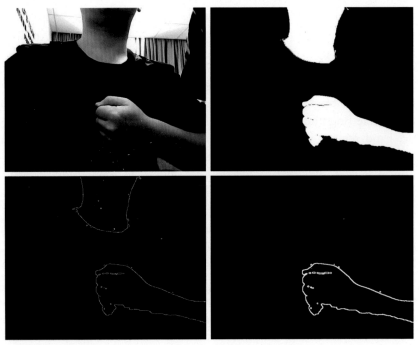

Figure 3.1 Example of gesture extraction results using skin color and Canny edge operator.

3.1.1.2 Active contour model-based segmentation

The active contour model is an energy functional-based approach that has significantly advanced traditional image segmentation and boundary extraction techniques. The main principle of the segmentation method is to use continuous curves to express the target edges. In this process, the first step is to provide an initial contour position in the image that will be segmented. The contour position is determined by a set of control points: $\mathbf{v}(s) = [x(s), y(s)]$ ($s \in [0, 1]$), where $x(s)$ and $y(s)$ represent the horizontal and vertical coordinate positions of each point in the image. s is an independent variable that describes the boundary in the form of a Fourier transform, so the segmentation process is transformed into a process of solving the minimum value of the energy functional, that is, when the function obtains the minimum value, the contour position is obtained by segmentation. The energy function of the active contour model can be further divided into two parts: internal energy functions and external energy functions. The internal energy function ensures the smoothness and continuity of the contour, and the external energy function controls the contour to converge toward the actual segmentation position. It only takes the local features of the image, such as the gradient of the control point or the location of the connection line [4]. The energy function of the active contour model can be formally described as:

$$E_{total} = \int_s \left(\alpha \left| \frac{\partial}{\partial s} \mathbf{v} \right|^2 + \beta \left| \frac{\partial^2}{\partial s^2} \mathbf{v} \right|^2 + E_{ext}(\mathbf{v}(s)) \right) ds \qquad (3.1)$$

The first term constitutes the modulus of the first derivative of $\mathbf{v}$, named elastic energy. The second term composes the modulus of the second derivative of $\mathbf{v}$, named bending energy. The third term represents external energy, defined as:

$$E_{ext}(\mathbf{v}(s)) = P(\mathbf{v}(s)) = -|\nabla I(\mathbf{v})|^2 \qquad (3.2)$$

Researchers commonly extract the hand outline via active contour models, subsequently segmenting the hand region bounded by the contour. For example, Wang Heng [2] utilizes an adaptive active contour model based on a level set to extract gesture contours, with results depicted in Fig. 3.2.

3.1.2 Motion analysis-based segmentation methods

Beyond image-based gestures, practical gesture recognition tasks require processing continuous gesture changes, necessitating the extension of hand segmentation from individual images to continuous video sequences.

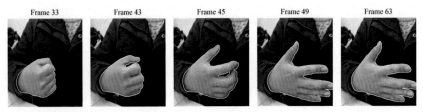

Figure 3.2 Extraction of hand regions across frames using level set-based active contour model.

Additional irrelevant factors, including lighting and background variations, affect segmentation, potentially reducing accuracy. Consequently, temporally changing information warrants consideration when performing hand region segmentation on dynamic video streams. Current video-based hand segmentation methods primarily encompass background subtraction-based segmentation, the interframe difference threshold–based method, and optical flow field–driven segmentation.

3.1.2.1 Background subtraction-based segmentation

The background subtraction-based segmentation method [5] first constructs a background image using multiple images or standalone background images. Subsequently, the current frame is subtracted from this background image to eliminate the background, followed by setting a threshold to achieve target segmentation. The principle and implementation of background subtraction segmentation remain relatively straightforward. However, based on background invariance, this technique proves more applicable when backgrounds are relatively uncluttered without external influences. As shown in Fig. 3.3, despite roughly outlining the human body, background subtraction fails upon camera displacement, producing differences in shifted regions, such as window frames. Additionally, when background and target brightness resemble each other, as with similarly colored skirting lines and clothing, subtraction cannot yield correct segmentation.

3.1.2.2 Interframe difference threshold-based method

The interframe difference threshold–based method [6] is a classic target segmentation method. Its principle proves similar to background subtraction, with both relying on background invariance. Specifically, for absent moving objects across video frames, only minor differences should manifest between consecutive frames. However, moving objects engender salient interframe differences. In practice, the most common approach is

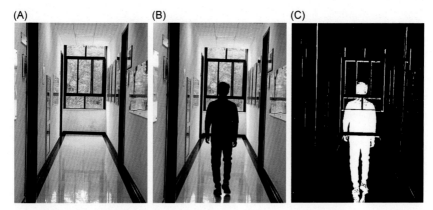

Figure 3.3 Effect of segmentation background subtraction. (A) Background. (B) People moving in the scene. (C) Segmentation effect.

to use adjacent frames in the video sequence, typically two to five, to undergo subtraction to obtain the absolute value of the brightness difference. Since the threshold critically distinguishes frame differences as either noise or moving targets, appropriate threshold selection remains imperative, commonly through experimental tuning. Improper thresholding risks segmentation noise or misjudging targets. Fig. 3.4 exhibits moving object segmentation using an interframe difference threshold of 0.5. While largely outlining the human body, this method fails to account for subtle changes, such as the performer's right foot.

3.1.2.3 Optical flow field-driven segmentation

The optical flow algorithm, proposed by Horn and Schunck [7] in 1981, is a method that calculates motion information of objects by analyzing temporal variations of pixels at the same location across an image sequence. Fundamentally, optical flow constitutes relative movement stemming from the foreground target, imaging device, or joint motion within a scene. Chapter 6 elaborates on optical flow modality applications in gesture recognition.

The crux of optical flow-based segmentation involves determining the target optical flow. According to the grayscale invariance principles, the fundamental optical flow equation emerges, which is formally expressed as:

$$I_x u + I_y v + I_t = 0 \tag{3.3}$$

where u and v represent the speeds of optical flow along the x-axis and y-axis, respectively, and I represents the light intensity. All gradient-based optical flow

Figure 3.4 Interframe differential motion for moving object segmentation effect.

algorithms rely on this formula. The establishment of this equation is based on three assumptions: (1) brightness consistency between reference and current frames; (2) continuous temporal relationship between reference and current frames; and (3) consistent motion among pixels within the same image.

The optical flow fields leverage image plane brightness changes to characterize object motion states. When there are moving objects in the scene, since the target moves relative to the background, its motion vector must be different from the background motion vector. Optical flow features can thus be obtained, and the moving target can be segmented [8]. Fig. 3.5 exemplifies utilizing optical flow features to highlight motion areas within the AUTSL dataset [9].

3.1.3 Skin color feature-based segmentation methods

Skin color feature-based segmentation methods primarily utilize hand skin color information to delineate hand regions. Given insensitivity to motion, skin color cues frequently aid hand area segmentation tasks.

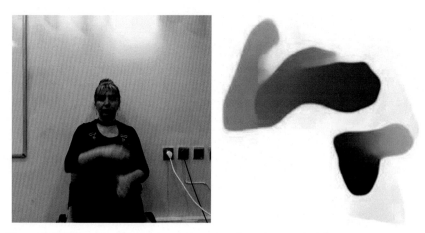

Figure 3.5 Effect of segmenting moving areas based on optical flow.

Skin color feature-based segmentation is divided into physics-based and statistics-based methods. Physics-based methods typically achieve segmentation by adaptively setting skin color thresholds. Generally, since head location is readily discernible by shape, adaptive segmentation often derives thresholds from the head region. Initially, a threshold based on the color of the head region is set, and the largest three regions segmented based on this threshold represent the positions of the head and both hands, thereby segmenting the hand region. Statistical-based methods leverage skin color models for detection and segmentation, comprising two steps: color space selection and skin color modeling. The selection of the color space is generally to find a color space that can distinguish hand skin and other areas effectively. It is usually selected from color spaces such as RGB, YCbCr, HSV, and HIS. Modeling skin color mainly includes nonparametric histogram statistics and pixel classification (i.e., distinguishing whether it is a skin area). As shown in Fig. 3.6, Wang Heng [2] segments hands by thresholding and marking skin regions in YCbCr space. In practice, segmentation methods based on skin color characteristics are closely linked to factors such as choice of color space, series of color levels, and pixel classification methods. These methods often require unobstructed visibility of both hands and are commonly used in combination with other techniques.

3.1.4 Summary

Hand area segmentation plays an important role in early gesture recognition methods. The quality of gesture segmentation directly affects the

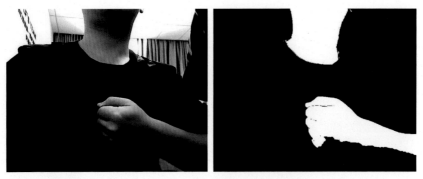

Figure 3.6 Example of segmentation effect based on skin color.

accuracy of gesture recognition results. Each method introduced above has its advantages, but there are also certain limitations. For example, for images with simple backgrounds, edge detection or threshold methods alone can achieve good results. However, for complex images, it might be necessary to combine several different methods to effectively segment hand regions from the background.

3.2 Gesture feature extraction

Representing gestures through appropriate features is a crucial step in gesture recognition. To describe the changes in gestures more accurately, researchers have proposed a variety of handcrafted features. In addition to the local features, such as skin color and edges mentioned in the previous section, commonly used gesture features also include features extracted directly from the entire image. The following section will provide individual introductions to these features and their extraction methods.

3.2.1 Haar-like features

Haar-like features identify objects by computing pixel brightness ratios within image regions, named for similarity to the Haar wavelet transform. Initially proposed by Papageorgiou et al. [10] at the 1998 ICCV conference, this feature was further improved by Lienhart et al. [11] who introduced the 45-degree diagonal feature. As shown in Fig. 3.7, Haar-like features can be divided into linear features, center features, and diagonal features based on the relationship between black and white rectangles in the template. When employing this feature for object recognition, the calculated Haar-like feature values are compared with a predefined

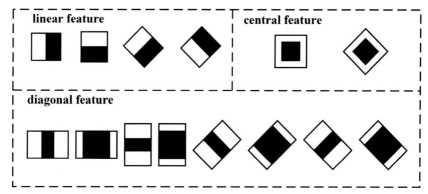

Figure 3.7 Haar-like feature template [11].

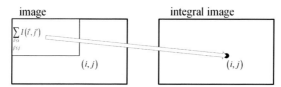

Figure 3.8 Schematic diagram of integral diagram construction.

threshold to distinguish between the target area and the nontarget area. Since a single Haar-like feature results in a weak classifier, the AdaBoost concept is often utilized. Numerous weak classifiers are cascaded to form a robust classifier, thereby combining several Haar-like feature templates. The basic template comprises black and white rectangles, valued at 0 and 1, respectively. For an image, the sliding window Haar-like feature equals the summed brightness across white rectangles minus the black rectangle summed brightness. Although the Haar-like feature can reflect the gray-scale changes of the image, this feature is only sensitive to some simple graphic structures corresponding to the template, such as edges, so it can only describe specific linear structures, central structures, diagonal structures, etc. However, because the Haar-like feature calculates the gray level difference between white and black rectangles instead of pixel-by-pixel calculation, this feature is highly robust to noise and illumination changes.

Haar-like feature computation relies on integral images [10], accumulating spatial pixels to represent global information. As shown in Fig. 3.8, the value of each point (i,j) in the integral map is the sum of all the values of the rectangular area in the upper left corner of the corresponding position in the original image. Therefore, when calculating the sum of pixel values in a certain region, the image position can be directly used to index the integral map without recalculating the sum of pixels in this area. Using the integral graph to obtain the Haar-like eigenvalues only requires traversing the image once, which greatly improves the efficiency of calculating the Haar-like eigenvalues of the image. Hence, the initial step in extracting Haar-like features involves computing the integral image.

As mentioned above, the value of the integral map at position $SAT(i,j)$ is the sum of all pixels in the upper left direction of the original image (i,j), specifically defined as:

$$SAT(i,j) = \sum_{\substack{i' \leq i \\ j' \leq j}} I(i',j') \tag{3.4}$$

It can be further described in a recursive form as:

$$SAT(i,j) = SAT(i-1,j) + SAT(i,j-1) + I(i,j) - SAT(i-1,j-1)$$
$$SAT(1,1) = I(1,1)$$

$$(3.5)$$

When performing gesture recognition through Haar-like features, a common approach is to regard the hand area as a cuboid surrounded by five cylinders. Both the prism and cylinders exhibit light–dark contrasts, with variations in contrast for different template sizes. Consequently, the cascading classification results obtained from Haar-like features can be effectively employed for the extraction of gesture characteristics. In 2015, Hsieh et al. [12] used Haar-like feature pairs for gesture recognition. For image-based gestures, Hsieh et al. directly used the template (Fig. 3.9A) to extract Haar-like features from the grayscale image and then used the extracted results to classify the two gestures of clenched fists and open palms and perform gestures based on this identification.

Figure 3.9 Implementing image-based gesture recognition using Haar-like features.

For the real-time video-based gesture recognition problem, Hsieh et al. reduced each frame of an image into a 24 × 32 matrix and used it to generate a motion history image (MHI). They use the feature template in Fig. 3.10 to identify the direction of hand displacement changes in the image and finally determine the category result of the video-based hand gesture. The relevant original pictures, MHI, and template pictures are shown in Fig. 3.11.

For some asymmetric gestures, Ghafouri et al. [13] designed new Haar-like features that are roughly proportional to the hand area and added these

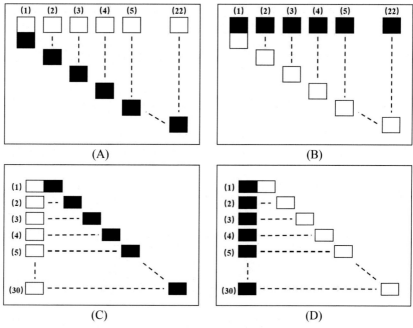

Figure 3.10 Haar-like template for detecting gesture movement direction [12].

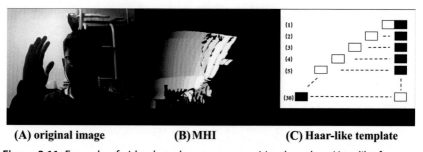

(A) original image   **(B) MHI**   **(C) Haar-like template**

Figure 3.11 Example of video-based gesture recognition based on Haar-like features.

features to the previous Haar-like feature templates. Fig. 3.12 shows such a new set of templates. Notably, since this newly designed Haar-like feature lacks symmetry, the eigenvalues cannot be calculated using the integral image mentioned above; instead, they need to be calculated by analyzing the difference between the convolution results of the black and white areas.

3.2.2 Local binary pattern features

Local Binary Pattern (LBP) is a descriptor of the local texture features of an image, as proposed by Ojala and Pietikäinen [14] in 1999. Fig. 3.13 defines the LBP operator. For each pixel, within its 3×3 square area, the eight surrounding pixels will be compared with its brightness values. If the brightness value of a pixel at a peripheral position is greater than the brightness value of a pixel at the center position, the position is marked as 1, otherwise it is marked as 0. This comparison generates an 8-bit binary value in a window called the LBP value. Since the LBP value can represent the light and dark relationship of the area, this value can be used to reflect the texture information of the area. Usually, 8-bit binary numbers are converted into decimal LBP codes (the value range is 0−255) for easy calculation.

It can be seen from the definition of LBP that the LBP operator has grayscale invariance, that is, no matter how the pixel value changes, as long as it is higher than the pixel value of the center pixel, the position

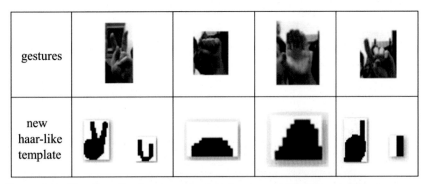

Figure 3.12 New Haar-like features template for asymmetric gestures [13].

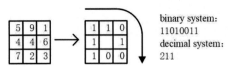

Figure 3.13 LBP calculation rules.

will be marked as 1, and vice versa. However, this operator lacks rotation invariance because the image rotation will cause the absolute starting position of LBP in the window to change, resulting in different LBP values.

However, since the LBP operator only calculates in a 3×3 neighborhood, it can be seen from the definition of the LBP operator that when the image is scaled and rotated, the LBP feature becomes unreliable. Furthermore, using LBP as the target feature is viable when the texture information across the entire image remains consistent; it becomes less applicable when the target exhibits rich texture amidst complex background edge information. In gesture recognition tasks, the boundary between the hand and background may not be obvious, so in general, LBP features usually need to be combined with other features for gesture recognition tasks.

As mentioned, due to the typically complex nature of background edge information in images, the grayscale differences within each window tend to be intricate, making it challenging to derive accurate LBP feature information. Therefore, Zhang et al. [15] combined the two features of HOG (histogram of oriented gradient) and LBP to complete the gesture recognition task. The HOG feature is the image gray gradient feature (see Section 3.2.5 for a detailed introduction to the HOG feature). To fuse the two features, Zhang et al. first extracted the reconstructed HOG features and subsequently used uniform LBP to calculate the histogram of each block. This method can reduce the impact of high-frequency noise. The steps to extract uniform LBP features are as follows:

1. Divide the image into several cells according to the feature extraction requirements, with the division basis determined by the characteristics of the recognition task.
2. Calculate the LBP feature value of each pixel position in each cell according to the method described above.
3. Perform histogram statistics based on image area division and calculate LBP feature values, that is, counting the number of occurrences of each LBP feature value in each cell, and normalizing the histogram.
4. Combine the statistical histogram features in each cell of the entire image into a vector, thereby obtaining the LBP feature vector of the entire image.

Additionally, Wang et al. [16] also combined uniform LBP and principal component analysis (PCA) to extract gesture features and reduce dimensions to achieve gesture recognition. This method first uses image preprocessing algorithms, including YUV color space segmentation and connected component detection, to obtain the complete hand region in the image. Afterward, the uniform LBP features of the hand region are extracted, and PCA is utilized for dimension reduction, decreasing the computational overhead of the algorithm. Finally, support vector machines are used for classification, achieving the ultimate recognition.

3.2.3 SIFT features

Scale-invariant feature transform (SIFT) is a local feature descriptor, as proposed by Lowe [17] in 1999 and further developed and improved in 2004 [18]. Compared with the Haar-like and LBP features introduced in the previous two sections, SIFT features are more complex, and the affine transformation of the image is more stable. SIFT features remain stable even if the image undergoes transformations, such as translation, scaling, and rotation. For this reason, SIFT features are widely used to deal with the matching problem between two images. Specific to the task of gesture recognition, due to the different personal habits of performers, the same gesture often has differences in scale (mainly due to the distance between the performer's hand and the camera), angle, and position. SIFT mainly utilizes some "stable" feature points, such as corner points, edge points, bright spots in dark areas, and dark points in bright areas, because they will not change due to illumination, noise, and affine transformation. Therefore, SIFT can achieve better results in gesture recognition problems. Generally speaking, SIFT features have the following characteristics:

1. Stable features: It has translation, rotation, and scale invariance and can avoid interference such as occlusion and noise to a certain extent.
2. Rich information: This feature can achieve fast and accurate matching in a massive feature library.
3. Quantity: Even if there are only a few objects in the image, sufficient SIFT feature vectors can be extracted.
4. Fast extraction: The optimized algorithm based on SIFT features can achieve real-time speed.
5. Strong scalability: SIFT features can be used not only alone but also in combination with other features.
   The generation of SIFT features generally includes the following steps.

3.2.3.1 Build Gaussian difference pyramid

To ensure the scale invariance of features, features are generally represented by the Gaussian Pyramid. Building a Gaussian pyramid of an image requires downsampling the image and filtering with different Gaussian kernels at the same scale. The process is shown in Fig. 3.14.

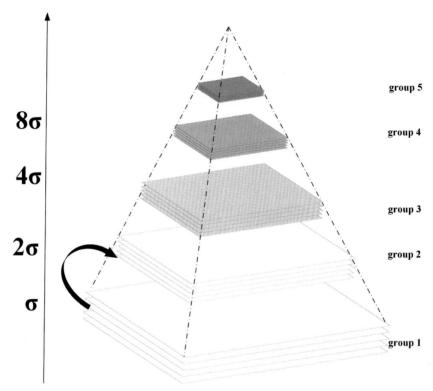

Figure 3.14 Image Gaussian pyramid.

As shown in Fig. 3.14, when constructing the Gaussian pyramid of an image, the image is first sampled to obtain images of different scales. The sampling process is implemented through point-interval downsampling. For images at each sampling scale, convolution is first performed using Gaussian kernels with different parameters, with each convolved image called one layer. The multilayer images at each scale are collectively referred to as an octave. After obtaining the Gaussian pyramid, adjacent layers at the same positions in each octave of the Gaussian pyramid are subtracted to generate the Gaussian difference pyramid shown in Fig. 3.15.

3.2.3.2 Determine location of keypoints
3.2.3.2.1 Primary selection of keypoints
The key feature points of SIFT are stable feature points in the image that do not change due to factors such as affine transformation or noise. These

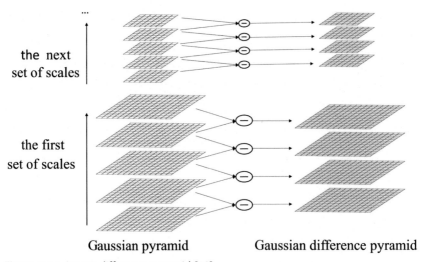

Gaussian pyramid   Gaussian difference pyramid

Figure 3.15 Image difference pyramid [18].

points are generally extreme points in the image. The differential pyramid is a gradient feature, so SIFT feature keypoints in the differential pyramid space are mainly local extreme points. The local extreme point is determined mainly by comparing the pixel at that location with the 26 adjacent points in space. Specifically, when a pixel is at an intermediate position within a scale of the Gaussian pyramid, comparisons are made between the images at different layers of the same scale. When it is located at the upper and lower boundaries of an octave of Gaussian pyramids, no comparison will be made. As shown in Fig. 3.16, any pixel in the image will be compared with 8 adjacent points around the pixel on the same layer. The pixel will also be compared with 9×2 points at corresponding positions on the upper and lower adjacent layers. So the pixel needs to be compared with a total of 26 points. The keypoints selected by this method are extreme points in different scale spaces of the pyramid and in the image itself. In gesture recognition, this initially determines the gesture edge points, or feature points, with a large difference between light and dark.

3.2.3.2.2 Adjustment of keypoints

The points obtained in the previous step are only rough local extreme points in the discrete space and are not necessarily real extreme points. To obtain more stable keypoints, it is necessary to use the difference function

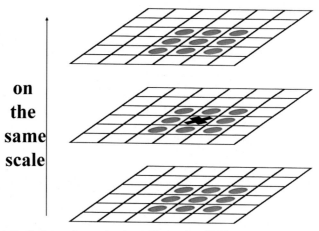

on the same scale

Figure 3.16 Preliminary determination of keypoints [18].

to perform curve interpolation in the scale space to adjust the keypoints. Specifically, it performs a quadratic Taylor expansion in the scale space of the difference pyramid, that is, it performs Taylor expansion at any extreme point (x_0, y_0, σ_0) and discards the second-order term, and determines the offset by finding the extreme value. After interpolation processing, the interpolation center of the interpolated keypoint is shifted to its neighboring points. Repeat the above steps and repeatedly interpolate at new positions until convergence, which can make the determined keypoints more stable. However, in this process, there may be points that have not converged within the set number of iterations or new extreme points that exceed the range of the image boundary, and such extreme points need to be removed.

3.2.3.2.3 Removal of edge effects

The difference calculation is equivalent to the first-order derivative of the image, which mainly describes the grayscale changes of the image. Therefore, the Gaussian difference operator will produce a strong edge response, but there will be unstable edge response points that need to be eliminated with the help of the second-order derivative. The second derivative of the image (the principal curvature) mainly describes the changes in the gray gradient of the image. If the principal curvature across the gradient direction is large at the extreme point position, and the principal curvature in the direction perpendicular to the gradient is small, such extreme points are unstable edge response points and need to be eliminated. The principal curvature is found through a Hessian matrix of **H**:

$$\mathbf{H} = \begin{bmatrix} \dfrac{\partial^2 f}{\partial x \partial x} & \dfrac{\partial^2 f}{\partial x \partial y} \\[2mm] \dfrac{\partial^2 f}{\partial x \partial y} & \dfrac{\partial^2 f}{\partial y \partial y} \end{bmatrix} \tag{3.6}$$

Because the principal curvature is proportional to the eigenvalues of the Hessian matrix **H**, the eigenvalues α and β of **H** represent the gradients in the x and y directions. Let α be the largest eigenvalue and β be the smallest eigenvalue, the edge-unstable feature point is exactly the point where α and β are significantly different. In other words, eliminating unstable edge effect points means retaining points with two eigenvalues that are equal or close to equal. This process can be obtained by using the trace of the matrix and the determinant of the matrix. The sum of the elements on the main diagonal of matrix **A** is called the trace of matrix **A**, denoted as tr(**A**). The trace is also the sum of all eigenvalues. The principal diagonal is the diagonal of the matrix from the top left to the bottom right. In this way, the principal curvature can be related to the trace of the matrix and the determinant of the matrix through the eigenvalues of the Hessian matrix.

Suppose the eigenvalues of **H** are α and β, and $\alpha > \beta$. Let $\alpha = r\beta$:

$$\frac{\text{tr}(\mathbf{H})^2}{\det(\mathbf{H})} = \frac{(\alpha+\beta)^2}{\alpha\beta} = \frac{(r\beta+\beta)^2}{r\beta^2} = \frac{(r+1)^2}{r} \tag{3.7}$$

where $\det(\mathbf{H})$ is the determinant of matrix **H**. Because $\alpha > \beta$, when $\alpha = r\beta$ and $r > 1$, the value of the above formula is minimum when the two eigenvalues of α and β are equal, namely when $r = 1$. And as the ratio of the two eigenvalues of α and β increases, the value of the above formula increases. As mentioned above, edge unstable points appear when α and β are very different. Therefore, the larger the value of the above formula, the greater the difference between the two eigenvalues of α and β. To remove such unstable edge response points, the ratio of the above formula is usually used to compare with the set threshold. When $\frac{\text{tr}(\mathbf{H})^2}{\det(\mathbf{H})} < \frac{(r+1)^2}{r}$ is satisfied, the requirement is met, where r is a custom parameter, generally $r = 10$.

3.2.3.3 Direction of keypoints

After the above steps, stable keypoints can be obtained. However, the keypoints will change with image rotation, lacking rotation invariance. To make the obtained SIFT rotationally invariant, it is necessary to assign a reference direction to each stable key point using local gradient features. For the keypoints detected in the Gaussian difference image pyramid, the gradient direction and amplitude of all pixels in a circle with the feature point as the center and a radius of 1.5 times the Gaussian filtered image scale are calculated. The gradient directions and gradient amplitudes of all pixels in the statistical area are implemented using histograms, with Gaussian weighting also applied during statistics collection. The gradient histogram is divided into 36 direction intervals from 0 degree to 360 degrees, with an interval of 10 degrees. The peak direction of the histogram represents the principal direction of the keypoint, and the subpeak direction of the histogram represents its auxiliary direction. However, the determination of the auxiliary direction needs to meet the requirement that the gradient amplitude be greater than or equal to 80% of the peak value. As shown in Fig. 3.17, after determining the main direction, the entire area within the filter radius will be rotated to the main direction.

3.2.3.4 Construction of keypoint descriptors

After determining the coordinates, scale, and direction of each keypoint in the previous three steps, the descriptor can then be obtained based on this information. Building keypoint descriptors and assigning directions to keypoints are complementary to each other. Because the SIFT feature finds the

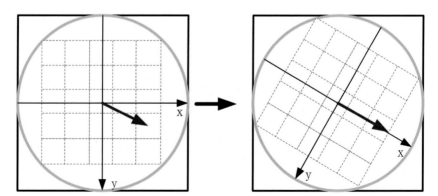

Figure 3.17 Directional rotation of SIFT feature keypoints.

main direction through gradient histogram statistics and turns the feature to the main direction, the keypoint description also uses the main direction as the starting direction to describe local features. The calculation methods of the two are similar. When constructing the keypoint descriptor, it is also necessary to count the pixels in the neighborhood of the keypoint to ensure that the generated descriptor is more stable. Therefore, constructing the keypoint descriptor first requires calculating the required area size. The calculation method of the area size is actually flexible. This section uses the following formula to calculate the required image area radius:

$$r = \frac{3\sigma \cdot \sqrt{2} \cdot (d-1)}{2} \tag{3.8}$$

where d represents the number of subregions, and the calculation result is rounded.

Lowe proposes [18] that the SIFT descriptor has the best discrimination when generating a 4×4 dimensional gradient direction histogram, namely $d = 4$. Taking Fig. 3.18 as an example and using the 8×8 neighborhood range as the feature description range, a 2×2 gradient histogram can be generated. Each histogram has 8 directions, that is, a $2 \times 2 \times 8$ dimensional feature vector is obtained. By analogy, to increase the robustness and antinoise ability of SIFT features, the range of feature description is set to 16×16, that is, a 4×4 gradient histogram is generated. Each gradient histogram also has 8 directions and thus obtains the $4 \times 4 \times 8$ dimensional SIFT feature vector.

Since SIFT has rotation, scale scaling, and brightness invariance, it is a very stable local feature. In pure gesture images, SIFT can stably obtain keypoints

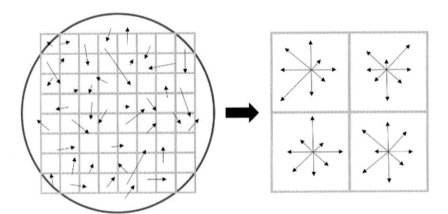

Figure 3.18 SIFT descriptor [18].

on finger edges. Therefore, SIFT features are also widely used in the gesture recognition field. As shown in Fig. 3.19, in 2012 Gurjal and Kunnur [19] first extracted the SIFT features of gesture images and then matched them with templates in the gesture template library to complete gesture recognition. In the process of keypoint extraction for gesture recognition, the direction assigned to the keypoint for each sample is obtained in the form of its gradient amplitude and Gaussian-weighted circular window weighting. Subsequently, the gradient direction histogram is used to obtain stable features in the local area, and the peak direction in the direction histogram is used as the dominant direction of the SIFT feature at that location. The direction of the location feature is the highest peak of the histogram, and any other local peak within 80% of the peak height is the direction of the feature point. If there are multiple peaks of similar magnitude, some points will be assigned multiple directions. A Gaussian distribution is fit to the three histogram values closest to each peak, with peak positions interpolated for better accuracy.

3.2.4 SURF features

Speeded-up robust feature (SURF) is a feature descriptor proposed by Bay et al. [20]. This feature descriptor is mainly used to detect, describe, and match local feature points of the image and add the scale factor when calculating the feature points. The extraction process of SURF can be regarded as an accelerated version of SIFT by approximating Laplacian with Gaussian to accelerate processing. However, SURF eschews direct Gaussian differentiation, instead deploying simplified templates for computation. The simplification of the filter template makes the calculation speed of SURF features several times faster than that of SIFT features, and the overall performance of SURF features is better. The most critical optimization is to use the integral graph in Hessian to accelerate the calculation. The SIFT algorithm builds a pyramid of an image, performs Gaussian filtering on each layer and

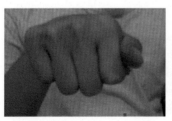

Figure 3.19 Gesture recognition process based on STFT features. (A) Input gestures. (B) SIFT features of gestures. (C) Recognition results.

obtains the image difference of the Gaussian to extract feature points. SURF leverages the Hessian matrix to extract feature points, so the construction of the Hessian matrix is the core of the SURF algorithm. We will detail the Hessian matrix construction below.

For a two-dimensional image, the first-order derivative constitutes grayscale change, that is, the grayscale gradient. The second-order derivative (Hessian matrix) represents the degree of gradient variation. The larger the second-order derivative is, the more likely the grayscale change is to be nonlinear, so the second-order matrix is used for abnormal point detection in the image. Formula (3.6) defines the Hessian matrix for an image pixel, characterizing surrounding gradient change rates. If the pixel value is an extreme value, the pixel is considered to be a stable edge point of the generated image. Similar to SIFT edge effect point removal, the Hessian matrix eigenvalues α and β denote gradients along the x and y directions. Let α be the maximum eigenvalue and β be the minimum one. Greater divergence between α and β implies larger pixel fluctuation, suggesting that the point is more likely to be an unstable point. This approach leverages the two eigenvalues α and β to quantify pixel stability, and the eigenvalues are multiplied to correlate the fluctuations with the value of the determinant. The details are as shown in Formula (3.9):

$$\det(\mathbf{H}) = \alpha\beta = \frac{\partial^2 f}{\partial x^2}\frac{\partial^2 f}{\partial y^2} - \left(\frac{\partial^2 f}{\partial x \partial y}\right)^2 \tag{3.9}$$

The specific calculation method of SURF features is similar to the basic process of the SIFT algorithm and can also be divided into four steps: constructing the scale space, locating keypoints, determining the direction of the feature points, and generating feature descriptors.

3.2.4.1 Construction of scale space
Similar to SIFT, the SURF scale space comprises O octaves of S layers. The difference is that the SIFT algorithm constructs an image pyramid, and the scales of different octaves of images are different (halving length and width between octaves). The images in the same octave are of the same scale, and the coefficients of the Gaussian kernel of images in different layers gradually increase. But in SURF, the same SURF octave scales remain constant; only Gaussian kernel coefficients between layers vary. So SURF actually builds a filter pyramid, avoiding the process of downsampling the image, and thus speeding up the extraction of features.

The Gaussian filters follow normal distributions, with coefficients decreasing from the center outward. To further accelerate processing, SURF substitutes box filters approximating the Gaussians when constructing scale space. Therefore, a weighting coefficient of 0.9 is multiplied on $\frac{\partial^2 f}{\partial x \partial y}$ during the calculation process to reduce the error caused by the box filter. Formula (3.9) becomes:

$$\det(\mathbf{H}) = \frac{\partial^2 f}{\partial x^2} \frac{\partial^2 f}{\partial y^2} - \left(0.9 \times \frac{\partial^2 f}{\partial x \partial y}\right)^2 \tag{3.10}$$

Two examples of substituting box filters for Gaussian filters are given in Fig. 3.20. The two images above the arrow show the results of applying a

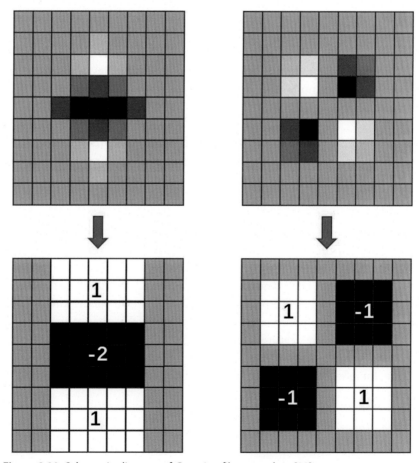

Figure 3.20 Schematic diagram of Gaussian filter template [20].

9×9 Gaussian filter template to find the second-order derivatives $\frac{\partial^2 f}{\partial y^2}$ and $\frac{\partial^2 f}{\partial x \partial y}$ on the image. The two images below the arrow show the approximation of the Gaussian filter using a box filter, where the pixel value of the gray part is 0, black part is -2, and white part is 1. This demonstrates that a more complex convolution filter can be converted to additions and subtractions between different image regions using a box filter, greatly simplifying the complexity of the problem. This can take advantage of the integral image and only requires several simple searches of the integral image to complete the operation, substantially accelerating the construction of the scale space.

3.2.4.2 Location of keypoints
SURF keypoint localization is similar to SIFT—compare each pixel after box filtering with its 26 neighbors in the spatial and scale neighborhoods to derive coarse points. The 3D quadratic difference method then iterates until convergence to obtain more stable feature points. Notably, unlike SIFT, SURF employs the Hessian determinant for keypoint selection, intrinsically accounting for edges without necessitating explicit edge response exclusion.

3.2.4.3 Determination of the direction of feature points
When determining the direction of feature points, similar to SIFT, SURF also assigns principal orientations to the feature points. However, unlike histogram-based gradient counting in pixel neighborhoods in SIFT, the principal direction of SURF counts Haar wavelet features in the circular neighborhood of feature points. Specifically, with the keypoint as the center, the sum of the Haar wavelet eigenvalues in the horizontal and vertical directions of all points in its circular neighborhood is calculated at intervals of a certain angle. Then Gaussian weight coefficients are assigned to these eigenvalues, so that the response contribution close to the feature point is larger, while the response contribution far away from the feature point is smaller. Finally, the features within a certain angle range are added to form a new vector, the entire circular area is traversed, and the direction of the longest vector as the principal direction of the feature point is selected.

3.2.4.4 Generation of feature descriptors
SURF descriptor construction requires an image Haar wavelet response calculation. When calculating the feature descriptor, a 4×4 pixel block is

drawn around the feature point, and the rectangular block is rotated to the direction of the main direction of the described feature point. The summation of the Haar response eigenvalues in the horizontal, vertical, horizontal absolute, and vertical absolute directions within the block is subsequently computed for the final descriptor values [21]. The resulting SURF feature descriptor not only has scale and rotation invariance but also illumination invariance.

The use of SURF features in gesture recognition is also similar to SIFT. In 2011, Bao et al. [22] used SURF features to track hand movements. First, since the feature points will not remain unchanged throughout the gesture sequence, the algorithm focuses on pairing and connecting the matching feature points between adjacent frames to reflect the general movement direction of the gesture. Thus, the algorithm classifies the gesture based on the movement mode of the gesture. Subsequently, the principal motion direction is calculated and selected as the motion feature of the gesture representation. Then, the robust and efficient SURF algorithm is used to extract significant feature points to ensure that the overall motion of the matching SURF points in adjacent frames can accurately represent the gesture motion. The principal motion direction of the matched SURF feature points in adjacent frames is used to help describe the hand trajectory. After dynamic time warping (DTW) (to be introduced in Section 3.3.3), the video-based gesture model is constructed through a series of trajectory direction data streams. Finally, SURF correlation analysis enables data flow clustering for video-based gesture recognition.

3.2.5 Features of histogram of oriented gradient

The features of HOG were proposed by Dalal and Triggs [23] as an image feature descriptor. These features are obtained by calculating histograms of gradient orientations in local regions of the image. One characteristic of HOG features is that they remain invariant to geometric and photometric transformations. Since HOG features can represent both the contour information of gestures and are also robust to environmental changes, they have been widely used in image-based gesture recognition [13,15,24–26].

The main idea of HOG features is that the appearance and shape of local objects in an image can be characterized by the distribution of gradients or edge directions. This is because gradients exist primarily on the edges. In practice, the image is usually divided into small regions called cells, and the histogram of gradient directions (or edge directions) is calculated for each cell. To make the results more robust to illumination and shadowing, cells are grouped into larger blocks, and histogram contrast normalization is performed to achieve invariance. In addition to having a larger receptive field, adjacent blocks overlap, thus effectively utilizing information from adjacent pixels. These normalized blocks are called HOG descriptors. Combining all the HOG descriptors in the detection image forms the final HOG feature vector. The relationship between the image, cells, and blocks is shown in Fig. 3.21.

The specific steps for extracting HOG features are:

1. Grayscaling: This step is for color images. Since HOG features are texture features rather than color features, the color image is first converted to grayscale for ease of processing.
2. Brightness enhancement: This is usually achieved through gamma correction. Because human perception of brightness is not linearly proportional to the actual image brightness but rather a power function relationship, gamma correction also uses such a power function for implementation. The function can be formally described as:

$$L = P^{\gamma} \tag{3.11}$$

where L represents the brightness perceived by the human eye, that is, the gamma-corrected image; P represents the input image; and γ is the exponent of this power function, commonly taking a value of 2.2, namely the gamma value for gamma correction.

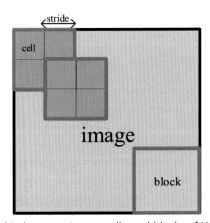

Figure 3.21 Relationship between image, cells, and blocks of HOG features.

3. Calculation of image pixel gradients: According to Eq. (3.12), the gradient values of the pixels are calculated separately in the horizontal and vertical directions, and the gradient magnitude and gradient direction of the pixel (x, y) are calculated accordingly.

$$G_x(x, y) = I(x + 1, y) - I(x - 1, y)$$
$$G_y(x, y) = I(x, y + 1) - I(x, y - 1)$$
$$G(x, y) = \sqrt{G_x(x, y)^2 + G_y(x, y)^2}$$
$$\theta(x, y) = \arctan\left(\frac{G_y(x, y)}{G_x(x, y)}\right)$$

(3.12)

where $G_x(\cdot)$ and $G_y(\cdot)$ represent the gradients in the horizontal and vertical directions; $I(\cdot)$ represents the brightness value of the pixel point; and θ represents the angle between the two directions.

4. Statistical analysis of gradient directions: First calculate the gradient direction and magnitude, then statistically analyze the gradient direction to obtain the gradient direction histogram of the entire image. In actual calculation, the entire image is divided into multiple blocks, each of which is divided into multiple cells, and then the gradient directions in each block and cell are statistically analyzed.

5. Contrast normalization: Due to local illumination changes and differences in contrast between foreground and background, gradient variations across the entire image can vary greatly. Therefore, normalization of the calculated histogram is required to balance it out. Since the L2 norm is simple and works relatively well for detection, it is generally used for normalization.

As mentioned above, HOG features have been widely used in various target detection and recognition tasks, including gesture recognition. Konečný et al. [24] observe dataset details such as the specific spatial positions of descriptors, especially the fact that user positions do not change within the same batch. Based on the prior knowledge that the performer's position generally does not change when demonstrating gestures, they assumed that important parts of the same gesture will also occur roughly in the same position, and they used HOG features to describe the positional information of gesture variations.

Konečný et al. [24] characterized the local appearance and shape of objects very well through the distribution of local grayscale gradients (or edges). In this method, the gradient directions are divided into 16 directions between 0 degree and 180 degrees. Histograms are computed using cell units of 40 × 40 pixels spatially pooled into larger overlapping blocks of 80 × 80 pixels. Except for the four cells on the image boundaries, each cell belongs to four blocks. Therefore, for each cell, four locally normalized histograms can be obtained, whose sum is taken as the final histogram for that cell. Notably, since histogram normalization cannot be directly performed on the image boundaries, gestures are generally unlikely to appear in those regions. For the convenience of implementation, Konečný et al. [24] omit those regions when extracting HOG features. In fact, through symmetric padding or zero padding of the boundary regions, the pixels in those areas can share the same neighborhood space as the central image pixels, thus enabling histogram normalization as well.

Fig. 3.22 shows an example of extracting HOG features from a gesture image. In the HOG feature map in Fig. 3.22B, it can be seen that the concentrated gradient direction range within each cell corresponds to the human body edges in Fig. 3.22A. The HOG features in box A correspond to the vertically downward area of the arm, with vertical gradients, while box B corresponds to the bent arm area, with gradients at an angle.

There are many other methods that use HOG features as edge descriptors in gesture recognition. Kaaniche et al. [25] constructed a HOG trajectory descriptor for gesture recognition. First, for each person in the scene, the authors select texture-based feature points to determine the texture areas for computing the HOG descriptors. Next, a neighborhood is defined for computing the 2D descriptors, and then these 2D HOG descriptors are tracked to build temporal HOG descriptors. Finally, the extracted local motion descriptors are classified using a classifier to learn a set of given gestures. Feng et al. [26] used support vector machines to train the HOG feature vectors. For parameter selection, Feng et al. chose an image size of 200×240, a window size of 28×28, a block size of 14×14, a stride of 7×7, a cell size of 7×7, and a histogram bin size of 9.

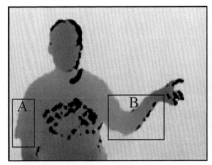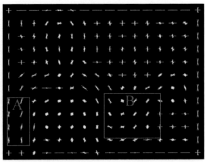

Figure 3.22 Examples of HOG feature extraction [24]. (A) Input image. (B) HOG feature map.

3.2.6 Features of histogram of oriented optical flow

The histogram of oriented optical flow (HOF) [27] is also a commonly used feature for gesture recognition. Similar to HOG, HOF features are also histogram-based, but weighted statistics are performed on optical flow directions rather than the original image. Optical flow can describe the changing direction of motion, but it is also very sensitive to background illumination and other variations. Therefore, a feature that can characterize temporal change information while being insensitive to illumination and other interfering factors is needed. The HOF feature happens to meet the above requirements. The calculation process of HOF features is similar to that of HOG, except that HOF analyzes optical flow statistically rather than gradient directions.

After obtaining the optical flow graph, the optical flow directions need to be statistically analyzed. The statistical process is also similar to the HOG statistics. As shown in Eq. (3.13), the angle between the optical flow vector and the horizontal axis is first calculated and then projected onto the corresponding histogram bin, weighted by the magnitude of that optical flow. Since the HOF histogram is obtained by weighting with optical flow magnitudes, small background noise has little effect on this feature.

$$\mathbf{v} = [x, y]^{\mathrm{T}} \quad \theta = \tan^{-1}(y/x) \tag{3.13}$$

As a feature that describes dynamic changes, HOF features are also extensively applied in the field of gesture recognition. In the method proposed by Konečný et al. [24], in addition to using HOG features to determine edge features, HOF features are also used to extract temporal features to determine interframe motion information. This is to determine the motion direction information of each block over time, thereby describing the changes in gestures in both spatial and temporal domains simultaneously.

3.2.7 Summary

In Sections 3.2.1−3.2.6, we discussed six manual features commonly utilized in gesture recognition. The selection of these features should be tailored to suit the specific requirements of the application and the characteristics of the dataset. For instance, image-based gesture recognition may benefit from features such as Haar-like, SIFT, SURF, and HOG, while video-based gestures typically require the incorporation of HOF features. Additionally, LBP features are frequently employed for texture analysis. In real-time applications, it is often advantageous to employ a combination of these features rather than relying on a single type to achieve a more detailed and accurate representation of gestures.

3.3 Gesture recognition

After preprocessing the input images or videos and extracting features from the hand regions, gesture recognition can be performed. Common gesture recognition methods include image-based gesture recognition through template matching, video-based gesture recognition through finite-state machine (FSM), DTW, etc.

3.3.1 Template matching

Template matching for images refers to obtaining the similarity between different images by comparing them and classifying them based on the similarities. Template matching is mainly used in image-based gesture recognition tasks by sliding the template over the captured source image to find regions similar to the template image. Template matching is usually based on grayscale correlation between images. Its basic principle is to scan pixel blocks in the image that are the same size as the template and compare each of them with the template according to a certain similarity metric. The mean squared error function is commonly used:

$$D = \sum_{m=1}^{M} \sum_{n=1}^{N} [S(m, n) - T(m, n)]^2 \qquad (3.14)$$

where m and n represent the horizontal and vertical coordinate indexes of the pixels; S and T represent the image block being tested and the template, respectively. Since directly matching the template with the entire image reduces efficiency, feature extraction or dimensionality reduction mentioned in the previous section can first be used to calculate feature similarities, which can greatly improve the efficiency of the matching algorithm.

Template matching has also found some applications in gesture recognition. Li [28] applies template matching for recognizing traffic police hand gestures. The method first performs background subtraction on the traffic police gesture images to segment out the hand regions. It then uses morphological processing and other methods to binarize the traffic police gesture images and obtain the corresponding hand contours. A skeletonization algorithm is then used to generate the final skeleton data for the hand regions. After obtaining the skeleton data, this method marks the pixel positions corresponding to the skeleton regions to generate a corresponding waveform graph and matches this waveform graph with each frame of the original video, based on which it identifies the frames corresponding to waveform peaks and valleys as key frames of the gesture. Finally, the Hausdorff distance template matching idea is used to match the feature parameters of the gesture to be identified for the prestored template feature parameters. Then, the algorithm calculates their Hausdorff distance and completes the final gesture recognition based on the distance difference with different templates.

3.3.2 Finite-state machine

A FSM, also known as a finite-state automaton is a mathematical model used to describe sequential logic by a finite number of states and actions that transition between them. In simple terms, state transitions require corresponding events to trigger corresponding actions. Take, for an example, riding an elevator. You need to press the elevator button (event) for the elevator to move to the corresponding floor and open the elevator door (action). The elevator door changes from closed (state) to open (transition). Therefore, the state machine requires four key concepts: state, event, action, and transition:

1. States: An FSM requires at least two states. For example, open and closed states of an automatic door.
2. Events: An event is the trigger condition or command to perform an operation. For the elevator door example above, pressing the open door button is an event.
3. Actions: After an event occurs, actions need to be performed. In the event of pressing the open door button, the corresponding action is to open the door.
4. Transitions: Refer to the transition from one state to another. For example, the door-opening process is a transition.

A gesture state can be considered as motion and velocity within a certain variance on a specified trajectory over time and space. In the training phase, states can be used to segment data and align them temporally. After obtaining the face and hand positions, gestures are modeled as state sequences in space and time. Each state is modeled as a multidimensional

Gaussian model. Assume the trajectory of a gesture consists of a set of points distributed in space. The distribution of the data can be represented by a set of Gaussian spatial blobs. A threshold is chosen to represent the allowed spatial variation for each state. These thresholds are calculated based on data and prior information about user gestures to determine the spatial variation of gestures.

Here, the state S can be denoted by a 5-tuple:

$$< \mu_s^p, \Sigma_s, d_s, T_s^{\min}, T_s^{\max} > \tag{3.15}$$

where μ_s^p is the centroid of the state; Σ_s is the spatial covariance matrix; d_s is the distance threshold; x^p is a point in 2D space, that is the input positional data; and $[T_s^{\min}, T_s^{\max}]$ is the duration time interval. A state and the spatio-temporal information of its adjacent states specify motion and velocity within a certain variance along a trajectory. The distance from the data point to state S is defined as the Mahalanobis distance:

$$D(x^p, S) = \sqrt{(x^p - \mu^p)\Sigma_s^{-1}(x^p - \mu^p)^T} \tag{3.16}$$

In training, there are specifically two phases:

Phase 1 (spatial clustering): Initially, the covariance of each state is assumed to be isotropic. Training starts offline from two state models and can use multiple samples of each gesture as training data, with the user continuously repeating these gestures on demand. During training, features are extracted using dynamic k-means to obtain the positional information of the head and hands, which is taken as one state. When the error changes by a very small amount, states are split at the maximum variance greater than the chosen threshold. Training stops when the variances of all states fall below the threshold. For the subset of data belonging to state S, the mean μ and variance σ^2 of data distance to the state center are computed. The distance threshold d_s of state S is set to $\mu + k\sigma$. After learning the spatial information, temporal alignment can be done.

Phase 2 (temporal alignment): Each data point is assigned a label corresponding to the state it belongs to. Thus we obtain a state sequence corresponding to the data sequence. From the temporal sequence of gesture states, the FSM structure of the gesture can be obtained. Currently the duration interval $[T_s^{\min}, T_s^{\max}]$ is set by computing the minimum and maximum number of samples in each state from the training data. Since the user can indefinitely remain in the first state of the FSM, $T_0^{\max}$ is set to infinity. After data alignment is complete, training can proceed.

Taking the "waving left hand" gesture as an example, as shown in Fig. 3.23, one cycle of its state sequence is [1 2 0 2 1]. According to the states contained in this cycle, a continuous sequence of gestures can be divided into samples of several states. For example, the sequence [1 1 1 2 2 2 2 0 0 0 0 2 2 2 1 1] contains five states, with 3, 4, 4, 3, and two samples per state, respectively. The number of samples in a state is proportional to the duration of that state. All gesture states are aligned in such a manner that different gestures share identical state sequences (as shown in Fig. 3.24), only with a different number of samples per state.

In practice, given that different states may vary in duration, a variable delay mechanism is often incorporated into the FSM to effectively manage these complexities. If a data sample does not fit the current state of

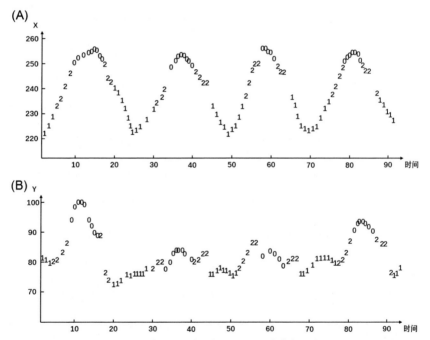

Figure 3.23 State sequence diagram for the "waving left hand" action [29]. (A) State sequence variation over time on x-axis.

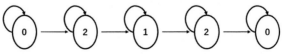

Figure 3.24 Transition process of gesture state sequence for the "waving left hand" gesture [29]. (B) State sequence variation over time on y-axis.

the FSM model, the model will remain in its current state and increase its own delay time value. If this delay time value exceeds a fixed small threshold, the FSM model is reset.

When all states of the FSM have been passed, it indicates that recognition has been completed. The FSM performs recognition by checking the current data sample and using the context information stored within it. The context information of a gesture recognizer g can be denoted as:

$$g = <S_k, t> \qquad (3.17)$$

where S_k is the current state of recognizer g; t is the time recognizer has stayed in S_k. Since the FSM has ordered state sequences, S_k stores the historical trajectory. When a new data sample x arrives, a state transition occurs if one of the following conditions is met:

$$\begin{cases} (D(x, s_{k+1}) \leq d_{k+1}) \& (t > t_k^{max}) \\ (D(x, s_{k+1}) \leq d_{k+1}) \& (D(x, s_{k+1}) \leq D(x, s_k)) \& (t > t_k^{max}) \\ (D(x, s_{k+1}) \leq d_{k+1}) \& (D(x, s_k) \geq d_k) \end{cases} \qquad (3.18)$$

Where $D(\cdot)$ is the Mahalanobis distance in Formula (3.16); d_k and d_{k+1} are the corresponding positional thresholds; and t_k^{max} is the corresponding temporal threshold. If the data sample happens to trigger more than one gesture recognizer, there is ambiguity, that is, it cannot be clearly judged which category the gesture belongs to. To resolve ambiguity, the category with the minimum average cumulative distance to the input gesture is chosen as the gesture category, calculated as:

$$\text{Gesture} = \underset{g}{\text{argmin}} \left(\sum_{i=1}^{n_g} \frac{D\left(x_i^p, s_{gi}\right)}{n_g} \right) \qquad (3.19)$$

where S_{gi} is the state of data sample x_i^p belonging to gesture g; n_g is the number of data points recognizer of gesture g has received up to the current time point.

In 2000, Hong et al. [29] proposed a method using FSMs for gesture recognition. They first defined each gesture as an ordered state sequence in space and time. Using the skin color based segmentation method mentioned in Section 3.1, the user's head and hands are located, and the 2D coordinates of the user's head and hand centers are taken as spatial features. Spatial information is then learned from the training data of given gestures, after which the data is aligned in time to construct FSM recognizers. Davis and Shah [30] applied a FSM to the field of gesture recognition. They proposed a model-based approach to recognize gestures. FSMs are used to model four different phases of generic gestures: (1) static start position; (2) steady motion of the hand and fingers until the end of the gesture; (3) static end position; and (4) steady return motion of the hand back to the start position.

3.3.3 Dynamic time warping

DTW can calculate the similarity between two time series, especially those with different lengths and rhythms. In gesture recognition, since the time lengths used by different performers to demonstrate the same gesture are not the same, DTW is very suitable for modeling the action variations of gestures.

When performing gesture recognition, DTW associates individual elements of the input gesture sequence with components of a class template sequence. Assume there are two different sequences, action sequence 1−1−3−3-2−4 and template sequence 1−3−2-2−4-4, each representing a gesture. If both represent the same gesture class, we want the calculated distance between them to be as small as possible when computing their distance, so that the probability of recognizing them as the same gesture will be greater. In this way, gestures of the same class can be classified together.

For the two sequences in the above example, calculating their Euclidean distance, which is the sum of the distances between each corresponding pair of points, yields a result of six. This leads to the conclusion that they are not the same gesture. However, this is not the case. DTW allows a point in one sequence to correspond to multiple continuous points in the other sequence (i.e., extending the time of the action represented by that point) and then calculates the sum of distances between corresponding points. As shown in Fig. 3.25, action 2(1) corresponds to actions 1(1) and 1(2), action 2(2) corresponds to actions 1(3) and 1(4), action 1(5) corresponds to actions 2(3) and 2(4), and action 1(6) corresponds to actions 2(5) and 2(6). From this, we can derive that the Euclidean distance is 0, indicating that the two are the same gesture. This result is consistent with the actual facts.

Corradini [31] determines the relative position of the face and hands by the outer contours of the head and shoulders, as well as visible skin regions and facial colors, thereby performing gesture recognition through DTW. First, they selected a suitable coordinate system by fixing the centroid of the head, then performed linear rescaling to avoid the effects of

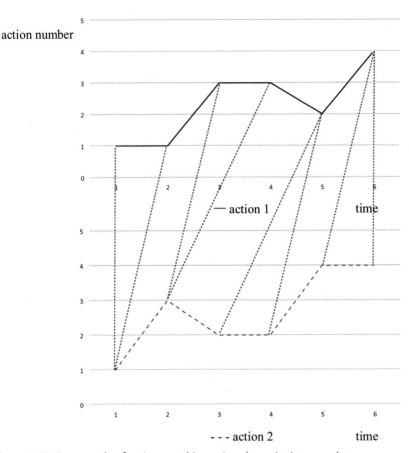

action number

— action 1   time

- - - action 2   time

Figure 3.25 An example of action matching using dynamic time warping.

image scale on the results. Afterward, the polar coordinates of the hands' centroids are computed together with the Cartesian coordinates of the hands' centroids along the x and y axes after velocity normalization. The coordinates are shown in Fig. 3.26.

In the image-based gesture recognition process, template matching is a simple implementation. However, for the temporal relationships in video-based gestures, template matching may result in inconsistencies in actions within each time segment due to differences in people's habits. For this, as shown in Fig. 3.27, Corradini et al. use numbers to indicate the relative durations of each action. The horizontal axis indicates time, and the vertical axis indicates action number. Video-based gesture recognition can first perform time warping and then matching. To reduce

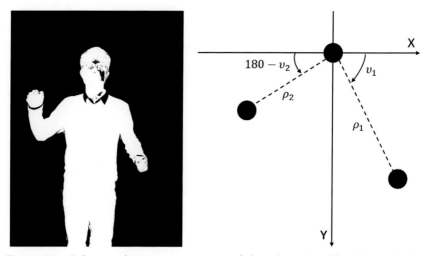

Figure 3.26 Polar coordinate representation of the relative head-hand spatial relationship [31].

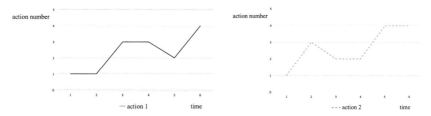

Figure 3.27 Examples showing relative durations of actions.

matching computation, the k–nearest neighbor is first used for preclassification, after determining which categories are more similar, matching is performed.

Many distance calculation methods are available when calculating the distance matrix between points of two sequences X and Y. Here they used the Euclidean distance d, where d is the distance between sequence points i and j on the two gesture sequences X and Y, calculated as:

$$d_{ij} = (x_i - y_i)^2 \tag{3.20}$$

$$X_i = \left\{ x_1, x_2, \ldots, x_{T_1} \right\}, 1 \le i \le T_1 \tag{3.21}$$

$$Y_j = \left\{ y_1, y_2, \ldots, y_{T_2} \right\}, 1 \le j \le T_2 \tag{3.22}$$

Where X_i and Y_j are two sequences of consecutive points; T_1 and T_2 are the times of the two sequences; and the distance between any two points of the two sequences constitutes the distance matrix. The distance between the two sequences is the minimum cumulative sum from the top left corner to the bottom right corner of the matrix. The cumulative distance S is calculated as:

$$S_{i,j} = \min \begin{cases} S_{i,j-1} + d \\ S_{i-1,j-1} + d \\ S_{i-1,j} + d \end{cases} \tag{3.23}$$

The cumulative distance is calculated recursively according to the recursive formula. In summary, the current cumulative sum equals the minimum cumulative sum of the previous step plus the current distance between the two sequence points. When calculating the cumulative sum, the cumulative sum of the previous step of the current two sequence points d can only be one of the following three:

1. The cumulative sum of the left adjacent element $(i, j - 1)$.
2. The cumulative sum of the upper adjacent element $(i - 1, j)$.
3. The cumulative sum of the upper left adjacent element $(i - 1, j - 1)$.

After the above analysis, the shortest path length can be calculated using a recursive algorithm, as shown in Eq. (3.24):

$$S_{\min}(i, j) = \min\{S_{\min}(i, j - 1), S_{\min}(i - 1, j), S_{\min}(i - 1, j - 1)\} + D(i, j)$$
$$S_{\min}(1, 1) = D(1, 1)$$

$$\tag{3.24}$$

Given action sequence A: 1−1−3−3-2−4 and template sequence B: 1−3−2-2−4-4, the DTW calculation process can be illustrated as shown in Fig. 3.28:

In this section, we explore three gesture recognition methods that have seen extensive application. In actual applications, the recognition method needs to be selected based on the application scenario, dataset characteristics, and feature extraction methods. For instance, image-based gestures can be effectively recognized using template matching, wherein the gesture that most closely resembles a predefined template is identified as the target gesture. In the case of video-based gestures, methods such as finite state machines and DTW are more appropriate. FSMs recognize by triggering gesture recognizers and select the gesture with the minimum average cumulative distance when there are multiple possibilities. DTW is similar to template matching, selecting the gesture with the minimum cumulative distance.

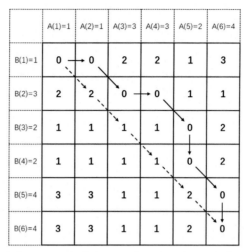

	A(1)=1	A(2)=1	A(3)=3	A(4)=3	A(5)=2	A(6)=4
B(1)=1	0	0	2	2	1	3
B(2)=3	2	2	0	0	1	1
B(3)=2	1	1	1	1	0	2
B(4)=2	1	1	1	1	0	2
B(5)=4	3	3	1	1	2	0
B(6)=4	3	3	1	1	2	0

Figure 3.28 Cumulative cost calculation results using dynamic time warping.

3.4 Summary

Gesture recognition has long been one of the main research areas in computer vision. Early methods were mostly based on steps of preprocessing, manual feature extraction, and gesture recognition. This chapter reviews some of the more commonly used and widely applied hand segmentation, feature extraction, and gesture recognition methods to provide readers with options to choose from based on their specific application scenarios.

References

[1] M. Sh, Y. Xiaodong, Research summary on gesture segmentation methods, Computer Optical Disk Software and Application 16 (11) (2013) 97−98 (莫舒, 杨小东. 手势分割方法研究综述. 计算机光盘软件与应用 16 (11) (2013) 97−98 (in Chinese)).

[2] W. Heng, Research on gesture tracking method based on adaptive active contour model. Lanzhou University of Technology, Gansu, 2012. (王衡. 基于自适应活动轮廓模型的手势跟踪方法研究[D]. 甘肃: 兰州理工大学, 2012 in Chinese).

[3] L. Shuiqiang, W. Yadong, C. Yonghui, Gesture recognition method based on geometric features, Computer Engineering and Design 35 (2) (2014) 636−640 (林水强, 吴亚东, 陈永辉. 基于几估特征的手势识别方法. 计算机工程与设计 35 (2) (2014) 636−640 in Chinese).

[4] M. Kass, A. Witkin, D. Terzopoulos, Snakes: active contour models, International Journal of Computer Vision 1 (4) (1988) 321−331.

[5] L. Wenping, H. Na, A new background subtraction moving target detection method, Computer Engineering and Application 47 (22) (2011). 175−175 (刘文萍, 贺娜. 一种新的背景减运动目标检测方法. 计算机工程与应用 47 (22) (2011) 175−175 in Chinese).

[6] S. Jiugen, C. Zhihui, Gesture segmentation based on motion history image and ellipse fitting, Computer Engineering and Application 50 (22) (2014) 199−202 (史久根, 陈志辉. 基于运动历史图像和椭圆拟合的手势分割. 计算机工程与应用 50 (22) (2014) 199−202 in Chinese).

[7] B.K.P. Horn, B.G. Schunck, Determining optical flow, Artificial Intelligence 17 (1−3) (1981) 185−203.

[8] X. Hong, Y. Bo, X. Wu, Moving target detection algorithm of LK optical flow method and three frame difference method, Applied Technology 43 (03) (2016) 23−27. + 33. (谢红,原博,解武.LK光流法和三帧差分法的运动目标检测算法.应用科技43　(03) (2016) 23−27 + 33 in Chinese).

[9] O.M. Sincan, H.Y. Keles, AUTSL: a large scale multi-modal turkish sign language dataset and baseline methods, IEEE Access 8 (2020) 181340−181355.

[10] C.P. Papageorgiou, M. Oren, T. Poggio, A general framework for object detection, Proceedings of International Conference on Computer Vision, IEEE, 1998, pp. 555−562.

[11] R. Lienhart, J. Maydt, An extended set of haar-like features for rapid object detection, Proceedings of International Conference on Image Processing, IEEE, 2002, pp. 900−901. I.

[12] C.C. Hsieh, D.H. Liou, Novel Haar features for real-time hand gesture recognition using SVM, Journal of Real-Time Image Processing 10 (2) (2015) 357−370.

[13] S. Ghafouri, H. Seyedarabi, Hybrid method for hand gesture recognition based on combination of Haar-like and HOG features, in: Proceedings of Iranian Conference on Electrical Engineering, IEEE, 2013, pp. 1−4.

[14] T. Ojala, M. Pietikäinen, Unsupervised texture segmentation using feature distributions, Pattern Recognition 32 (3) (1999) 477−486.

[15] Z. Fan, L. Yue, Z. Chunyu et al. Hand gesture recognition based on HOG-LBP feature, in: Proceedings of IEEE International Instrumentation and Measurement Technology Conference, IEEE, 2018, pp. 1−6.

[16] W. Jingzhong, X. Xiaoqing, L. Meng, The study of gesture recognition based on SVM with LBP and PCA, Journal of Image and Graphics 3 (1) (2015) 16−19.

[17] D.G. Lowe, Object recognition from local scale-invariant features, in: Proceedings of IEEE International Conference on Computer Vision, IEEE, 2, 1999 pp. 1150−1157.

[18] D.G. Lowe, Distinctive image features from scale-invariant keypoints, International Journal of Computer Vision 60 (2) (2004) 91−110.

[19] P. Gurjal, K. Kunnur, Real time hand gesture recognition using SIFT, International Journal of Electronics and Electrical Engineering 2 (3) (2012) 19−33.

[20] H. Bay, T. Tuytelaars, L. Van Gool, Surf: speeded up robust features, in: Proceedings of European Conference on Computer Vision, Springer, 2006, pp. 404−417.

[21] F. Peng, M. Aidong, C. Mengyang, et al., Color-SURF: a surf descriptor with local kernel color histograms, in: Proceedings of IEEE International Conference on Network Infrastructure and Digital Content, IEEE, 2009, pp. 726−730.

[22] B. Jiatong, S. Aiguo, G. Yan, et al., Dynamic hand gesture recognition based on SURF tracking, in: Proceedings of International Conference on Electric Information and Control Engineering, IEEE, 2011, pp. 338−341.

[23] N. Dalal, B. Triggs, Histograms of oriented gradients for human detection, Proceedings of IEEE Conference on Computer Vision and Pattern Recognition, IEEE, 2005, pp. 886−893.

[24] J. Konečný, M. Hagara, One-shot-learning gesture recognition using hog-hof features, The Journal of Machine Learning Research 15 (1) (2014) 2513–2532.

[25] M.B. Kaaniche, F. Bremond, Tracking hog descriptors for gesture recognition, in: Proceedings of IEEE International Conference on Advanced Video and Signal Based Surveillance, IEEE, 2009, pp. 140–145.

[26] F. Kai-ping, Y. Fang., Static hand gesture recognition based on HOG characters and support vector machines, Proceedings of International Symposium on Instrumentation and Measurement, Sensor Network and Automation, IEEE, 2013, pp. 936–938.

[27] N. Dalal, B. Triggs, C. Schmid, Human detection using oriented histograms of flow and appearance, in: Proceedings of European Conference on Computer Vision, Springer, 2006, pp. 428–441.

[28] L. Wenjie, Traffic Command Gesture Recognition Based on Skeletonization and Template Matching. Zhejiang University of Technology, Zhejiang, 2011. (李文杰. 基于骨架化和模板匹配的交通指挥手势识别. 浙江: 浙江工业大学, 2011 in Chinese).

[29] H. Pengyu, M. Turk, T.S. Huang, Gesture modeling and recognition using finite state machines, in: Proceedings of IEEE International Conference on Automatic Face and Gesture Recognition, IEEE, 2000, pp. 410–415.

[30] J. Davis, M. Shah, Visual gesture recognition, IEE Proceedings—Vision, Image and Signal Processing 141 (2) (1994) 101–106.

[31] A. Corradini, Dynamic time warping for off-line recognition of a small gesture vocabulary, in: Proceedings of IEEE International Conference on Computer Vision Workshops, IEEE, 2001, pp. 82–89.

CHAPTER 4

Gesture recognition method based on convolutional neural network

A convolutional neural network (CNN) is a network model inspired by bionic biology. In the 1960s, while studying visual cells in cats, American biologists discovered that each visual cell of a cat only processes a small region of the image rather than the entire region. Based on this discovery, they proposed the concept of local receptive fields [1]. In 1982, Japanese scientists Fukushima and Miyake [2] first applied the concept of local receptive fields to CNN, thus reducing the number of neuron connections and lowering the complexity of the network. In 1998, Lecun et al. [3] from the University of Toronto applied CNN to the recognition of handwritten digits and achieved good recognition results. However, due to the large software and hardware resources required to train the neural network, it is difficult to apply CNN for some complex tasks. These drawbacks caused CNN to fall silent for a period of time. It was not until 2006 that, with the continuous development of software and hardware technology, it became possible to train the deep neural network, and the academic community began to study CNN again. In 2012, AlexNet, proposed by Krizhevsky et al. [4] based on CNN, won first place in the ImageNet large-scale visual recognition challenge (ILSVRC), far exceeding the second place based on traditional methods by more than ten percentage points. Because of this development, CNN has attracted widespread attention from computer vision researchers around the world.

In the 2014 ILSVRC competition, Szegedy et al. [5] from Google proposed GoogLeNet, which reduces the recognition error rate on the ImageNet dataset by 6.67% through the designing of multiscale convolution units to extract features of different scales. A year later, He et al. [6] from Microsoft proposed a new network initialization method and activation function, further reducing the error rate by two percentage points. Domestically, researchers have also conducted a lot of exploration on

Gesture Recognition
DOI: https://doi.org/10.1016/B978-0-443-28959-0.00007-8

CNN applications in computer vision. For the target instance segmentation task in the scenes, the Megvii Technology team proposed a new instance segmentation framework based on cascaded CNNs [7]. This framework learns contextual information through semantic segmentation subnetworks and uses multitask, multistage hybrid cascades to achieve the final segmentation. To address the problem of human body keypoint detection, the Megvii Technology team proposed a multistage pose estimation CNN [8]. Yang et al. from Beijing University of Posts and Telecommunications proposed an end-to-end CNN called Parsing R-CNN to achieve instance-level human body parsing [9], aiming at the problem of insufficient detailed features in human pose estimation. CNN has gradually occupied a dominant position in research in the field of computer vision.

4.1 Basic operations of deep convolutional neural network

4.1.1 Characteristics of convolutional neural network

Compared with the traditional neural network, CNN has greater advantages in processing image data. On the one hand, due to the simpler structure and fewer network parameters of CNN, it is easier to train. On the other hand, since the object of convolution operations is a local area in the image rather than a single pixel, CNN has invariance to geometric transformations of images (such as translation, rotation, etc.). These advantages are mainly attributed to the three major characteristics of CNN [10]:

4.1.1.1 Local connection

Images have the characteristic that the pixels that are close together have close relationships, while pixels that are farther apart have weaker correlations. This is the implication of the local receptive fields mentioned above. Therefore, based on the concept of local receptive fields, researchers have proposed a method of replacing the global perception method with a local perception method, that is, each neuron in the neural network only needs to receive local pixel information as input and then performs the processing at a higher level of the network. The layer integrates the local information processed by different neurons to obtain global information. Using this local connection method can significantly reduce the parameters of the network. For example, assuming that the input to the network is a grayscale image with a length and width of 1,000 pixels, the input data has a total of $10^3 \times 10^3 = 10^6$ pixels. If the hidden layer has 10^6 neurons, using the full connection there would be $10^6 \times 10^6 = 10^{12}$ connections; if using the local connection method with a receptive field size of $10 \times 10 = 100$ pixels, only $10^6 \times 10^2 = 10^8$ connections are needed, which is just one tenthousandth of the parameters compared with the full connection. The schematic diagram of the two connection methods is shown in Fig. 4.1.

4.1.1.2 Weight sharing

Even if CNN reduces the number of parameters from 10^{12} to 10^8 through a local connection, the number of parameters is still too large and needs to be further reduced. To achieve this goal, CNN also adopts a weight-sharing strategy. In the above locally connected network, the hidden layer has 10^6 neurons, and each neuron corresponds to 100 parameters. If the 100 parameters corresponding to these 10^6 neurons are all the same, the parameters of this layer will be reduced from 10^6 to 100. As shown in Fig. 4.2, in CNN using weight sharing, the number of network parameters is independent of the input image size and the number of hidden layer neurons but is only related to the size of the receptive field.

4.1.1.3 Downsampling

Downsampling is a way of integrating features from different locations in the image. It is generally implemented through a pooling layer in CNN. The downsampling operation can not only further reduce network training parameters but also decrease the impact of pixel value changes on the convolution results, further improving the generalization ability of the network.

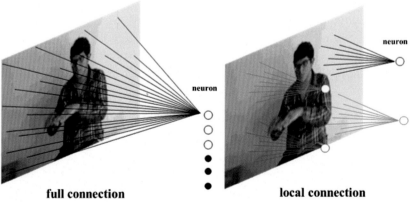

Figure 4.1 Schematic diagram of the difference between full connection mode and partial connection mode.

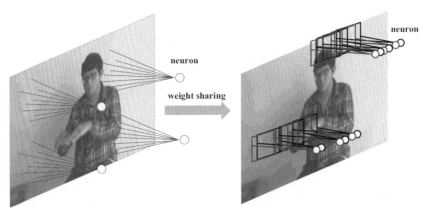

Figure 4.2 Weight sharing of convolutional neural networks.

4.1.2 Basic structure of convolutional network

Inspired by the neural network structure of animal brains, CNN is developed to analyze and process a large number of samples. Its main structure includes the input layer, convolution layer, activation function and pooling layer, etc.

4.1.2.1 Input layer

The input layer is generally used to process raw data or data after some simple preprocessing. The results corresponding to different modes of input data are also different. For audio or text data, a one-dimensional tensor can generally be obtained through the input layer. For image data, a 2D tensor can be obtained through the input layer. For video data, a three-dimensional tensor can be obtained through the input layer.

4.1.2.2 Convolutional layer

The convolutional layer is the most important structure in the CNN, which extracts the characteristics of the data through convolution operations. The convolution operation is usually implemented through the formula: Eq. (4.1):

$$o_{mn} = \mathrm{Conv}(x) = \sum_{i=1}^{I}\sum_{j=1}^{J} w_{ij}x_{m+i,n+j} + b \quad (1 \leq m \leq M, 1 \leq n \leq N) \quad (4.1)$$

where o_{mn} represents the pixel value of m-th row and n-th column in the output feature map; w_{ij} represents the value of i-th row and j-th column of the convolution kernel; $x_{m+i,n+j}$ represents the pixel value of the input feature at the convolution position; I and J represents the length and width of the convolution kernel, respectively; b represents the bias term of the convolution operation; M and N represent the length and width of the output feature map, respectively. The process of convolution operation is shown in Fig. 4.3.

Normally, since one convolution kernel can only extract one feature, to obtain multiple features of the data, multiple convolution kernels are generally used to perform convolution operations.

4.1.2.3 Activation function of convolutional neural network

The activation function is a function that maps the input of a neuron to the output, usually located after the convolutional layer. The activation function plays a very important role in CNN when processing complex nonlinear relationships. Since the convolution operation itself is linear, in this case, there is a linear relationship between layers. Therefore, no matter how many network layers there are, the output is a linear combination of the inputs. The activation function introduces nonlinear factors into CNN, improves the expression ability of CNN, and enables it to solve more complex problems.

Common activation functions include the sigmoid function, tanh function, and ReLU function. The curves of these three functions are shown in Fig. 4.4. These three activation functions will be introduced separately below.

4.1.2.3.1 Sigmoid function

The sigmoid function is a commonly used activation function. This function can be expressed as:

$$f(x) = \frac{1}{1 + e^{-x}} \tag{4.2}$$

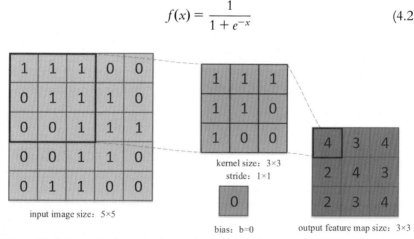

Figure 4.3 Schematic diagram of convolution operation.

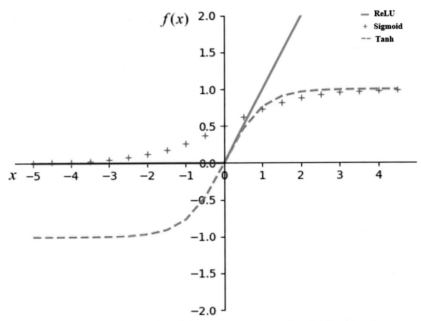

Figure 4.4 Function curve graphs of three commonly used activation functions.

As shown by the dotted line in Fig. 4.4, the sigmoid function can map any real value to the [0,1] interval. However, when the value is close to 0 or 1, the derivative value of this function is small. When there are many layers in CNN after the accumulation of multiple backward propagations, the gradient of the network will be very close to 0, resulting in the vanishing gradient problem. Because the value range of the sigmoid function is not zero-centered, its convergence efficiency will be affected. In addition, since its analytical formula contains power operations, it takes up more time to solve and increases the training cost of the network. Therefore, its role as an activation function has been gradually weakened. But for some special output requirements, such as limiting the output range to [0,1], the sigmoid function still plays an important role.

4.1.2.3.2 Tanh function
The form of the tanh function is as follows:

$$f(x) = \frac{e^x - e^{-x}}{e^x + e^{-x}} \tag{4.3}$$

The tanh function was proposed mainly to solve the problem that the sigmoid function is not zero-centered. However, as shown by the dashed curve in Fig. 4.4, the shape of the tanh function is similar to the sigmoid function, and the derivative at the boundary of the function is still small, which will also lead to the vanishing gradient problem, so this function has not been widely used either.

4.1.2.3.3 Rectified linear unit function

The ReLU (rectified linear unit) function [11] is a more commonly used activation function in recent years. Its expression is as follows:

$$f(x) = \begin{cases} x & x \geq 0 \\ 0 & x < 0 \end{cases} \tag{4.4}$$

The ReLU function takes the larger value between the input and 0. Although the form of this function is very simple, as shown by the solid line in Fig. 4.4, this function solves the vanishing gradient problem of the above two activation functions and is fast in calculation and easy to converge. Therefore, it is widely used in CNN.

In general, both the sigmoid and tanh functions have the vanishing gradient problem, and their analytical function formulas contain exponential operations; while the ReLU function can not only solve the vanishing gradient problem, it also needs to complete a threshold judgment once during the operation, thus involving a very small amount of calculation. In addition, ReLU sets the output of some neurons to 0, which improves the sparse expression ability of CNN and avoids the overfitting problem.

4.1.2.4 Pooling layer

A pooling operation is a type of downsampling. Adding a pooling layer to the network can further abstract features, enlarge the receptive field, and reduce the number of network parameters, thus lowering the difficulty of network training. Common pooling methods include average pooling and maximum pooling [12]. For each sampling area in the image, the average pooling method outputs the average value of the area, so it has a better effect of retaining the image background area. The maximum pooling method outputs the maximum value of the area, so it can better extract the high-frequency texture features of the area. Among these two pooling methods, the maximum pooling method is more widely used in CNN. Therefore, the maximum pooling method as an example is used to briefly introduce the operation of the pooling layer.

As shown in Fig. 4.5, assuming that the input feature is a 4 × 4 matrix, let the size of the maximum pooling (the size of the area involved in the

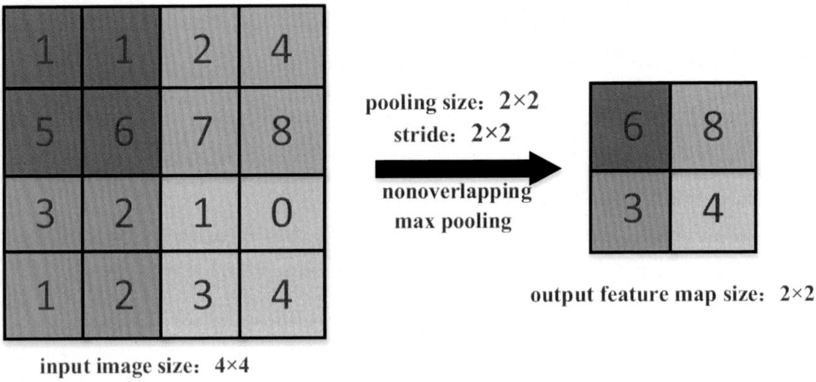

Figure 4.5 Schematic diagram of pooling operation.

pooling operation) be 2×2, and pooling stride (the number of pixels spanned by two adjacent pooling operations) be 2×2, that is, a nonoverlapping maximum pooling operation is implemented, and the size of the resulting output feature map is 2×2.

The process of max pooling can be formally described by the formula: Eq. (4.5):

$$o_{ij} = \text{MAXPOOL}(x) = \max_{m=1,2,\ldots,k_H} \max_{n=1,2,\ldots,k_W} x_{s_H \times i+m, s_W \times j+n} \qquad (4.5)$$

where o_{ij} is the pixel value of the feature map output by the maximum pooling operation in the i-th row and j-th column; x is the input feature map of the pooling operation; k_H and k_W are the height and width of the pooling area, respectively; m and n are the position indexes of the pixels involved in the pooling operation in x; and their value ranges $1, 2, \ldots, k_H$ and $1, 2, \ldots, k_W$. s_H and s_W are the vertical and horizontal strides, respectively.

4.1.3 Training process of convolutional neural network

There are mainly three training methods for CNN: supervised, unsupervised, and the combination of supervised and unsupervised (also called semisupervised). Among these three methods, the supervised approach is the most widely used in CNN. Therefore, this section mainly discusses methods of training CNN using the supervised approach.

When training CNN in a supervised manner, each training sample includes an input (usually represented in the form of a vector) and a label (also called ground truth). This label is also called a supervisory signal. In essence, the supervised training method is to train a network model based on the relationship between input data and labels in existing samples and use the model to give prediction results corresponding to unlabeled input data. Supervised training generally optimizes the network through stochastic gradient descent (SGD). SGD mainly includes two parts: forward propagation and backward propagation. Forward propagation calculates the output of each neuron layer by layer according to the computation methods of convolution, pooling, and other operations until the final prediction result of the network is obtained. The error between this prediction result and the label is calculated using a certain loss function. Backward propagation is in the opposite direction to the above process, using the chain rule to calculate the partial derivatives of the loss function by layer based on the weights and biases of the neurons in each layer. After the calculation is completed, the weights and biases of each layer are adjusted. Through multiple iterations of forward propagation and backward propagation processes, the training of CNN is completed. A simple example is given below to illustrate the specific processes of forward propagation and backward propagation.

Suppose there is an L-layers network that uses the mean square error function as the loss function. The error function can be expressed as:

$$\text{Loss}(\hat{y}, y) = \frac{1}{2}(\hat{y} - y)^2 \tag{4.6}$$

where $\hat{y}$ and y are the prediction results and corresponding labels of the network, respectively. During the forward propagation process, the output of the $l(1 < l \le L)$-th layer is as follows:

$$a^{(l)} = \sigma(z^{(l)}) = \sigma(W^{(l)} a^{(l-1)} + b^{(l)}) \tag{4.7}$$

where $a^{(l)}$ represents the output of the l-th layer and $a^{(l-1)}$ represents the input of the l-th layer, that is, the output of the $l-1$-th layer; σ represents the activation function; and $z^{(l)}$ represents the output of the neurons in this layer. In particular, when $l = L$, the output $o^{(L)}$ of this layer is the prediction result $\hat{y}$ of the entire network. During backward propagation, first calculate the gradient of the last layer of the network, that is, the L-th layer:

$$
\begin{aligned}
\delta^{(L)} &= \frac{\partial \text{Loss}(\hat{y}, y)}{\partial z^{(L)}} \\
&= \frac{\partial \text{Loss}(\hat{y}, y)}{\partial a^{(L)}} \frac{\partial a^{(L)}}{\partial z^{(L)}} \\
&= \frac{\partial \text{Loss}(\hat{y}, y)}{\partial a^{(L)}} \odot \sigma'(z^{(L)})
\end{aligned}
\tag{4.8}
$$

where $\odot$ represents the operation of calculating the Hadamard product; and $\sigma'(z^{(L)})$ represents the derivative of the function of the L-th layer of the network. According to the chain rule, the gradient of the l-th layer of the network can be deduced as follows:

$$\delta^{(l)} = \delta^{(l+1)} \frac{\partial z^{l+1}}{\partial z^l} = W^{(l+1)\mathrm{T}} \delta^{(l+1)} \odot \sigma'(z^{(l)}) \tag{4.9}$$

where the gradients of the parameters $W^{(l)}$ and $b^{(l)}$ for this layer can be obtained as:

$$\begin{aligned}
\delta_{W^{(l)}} &= \frac{\partial Loss(\hat{y}, y)}{\partial W^{(l)}} = \frac{\partial Loss(\hat{y}, y)}{\partial z^{(l)}} \frac{\partial z^{(l)}}{\partial W^{(l)}} = \delta^{(l)} (a^{(l-1)})^{\mathrm{T}} \\
\delta_{b^{(l)}} &= = \frac{\partial Loss(\hat{y}, y)}{\partial b^{(l)}} = \frac{\partial Loss(\hat{y}, y)}{\partial z^{(l)}} \frac{\partial z^{(l)}}{\partial b^{(l)}} = \delta^{(l)}
\end{aligned} \tag{4.10}$$

when the backward propagation is completed, the parameters can be updated layer by layer according to SGD. The updated formula is as follows:

$$\theta^{(l)} = \tilde{\theta}^{(l)} - \eta \delta_{\tilde{\theta}^{(l)}} \tag{4.11}$$

where $\tilde{\theta}^{(l)}$ represents the parameter of the l-th layer before the update, and $\theta^{(l)}$ represents the parameter of the layer after the update, which is equivalent to $(W^{(l)}, b^{(l)})$; η is the learning rate.

It is worth noting that since the pooling layer has no activation function, the output of the pooling layer is generally considered the same as the output of the neurons in that layer, that is, $\sigma(z) = z$. Also, since the pooling operation downsamples the input feature map, the layer needs to be restored to the same size as the input feature map through upsampling during backward propagation. For the convolutional layer, its backward propagation is achieved by flipping the convolution kernel 180 degrees.

4.2 Application of 2D convolutional neural network in gesture recognition

As mentioned above, CNN has a wide range of applications in computer vision. In the field of gesture recognition, researchers have also proposed a large number of CNN-based algorithms. This section will introduce several classic gesture recognition algorithms.

4.2.1 Two-stream network

The two-stream network is a CNN model for gesture and behavior recognition, as proposed by Simonyan and Zisserman [13]. As shown in Fig. 4.6, the two-stream network has two branches, both constituted by CNN. The spatial branch takes RGB data as input for extracting spatial features, including the position of the human body in each frame of the video. The temporal branch takes optical flow data as input for extracting temporal features, including the motion trajectories of various parts of the human body. After extracting spatial and temporal features through the two-branch network, the two-stream network fuses the features and uses the fused features to achieve gesture and behavior recognition.

4.2.2 Temporal segment network

In a two-stream network, the temporal information comes from the optical flow data processed by the temporal stream. Since optical flow data only considers the motion information between two adjacent frames, the temporal information that the two-stream network can process is also very limited. To effectively utilize the temporal information of the entire video, Wang et al. [14] proposed a temporal segment network (TSN) based on the two-stream network. Similar to the two-stream network, TSN uses RGB data and optical flow data as inputs to the spatial domain convolution subnetwork and the temporal convolution subnetwork, respectively. The difference is that TSN obtains a series of snippet sequences by segmentally sampling the entire video, and then uses these snippets as network input to obtain corresponding prediction results, and also uses the score fusion method to combine these prediction results. After fusion, the final prediction result of the entire video is obtained. The network structure of TSN is shown in Fig. 4.7.

When using TSN for gesture recognition, for a given video V, it is first divided into K segments $\{S_1, S_2, \cdots, S_K\}$. To ensure that the number

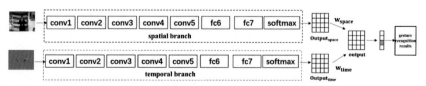

Figure 4.6 Network structure of two-stream network.

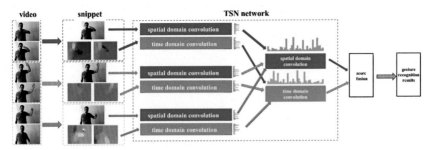

Figure 4.7 TSN network structure [14].

of video frames in each segment meets the requirements of the network, random sampling needs to be performed within each segment, thereby obtaining the segments of the input network $\{T_1, T_2, \cdots, T_K\}$. The network extracts features for each segment T_k $(k = 1, 2, \ldots, K)$ and outputs the probability that the segment represents a certain type of gesture. Subsequently, the category probabilities corresponding to these segments are integrated through the segment consensus function G, and finally, the recognition result of the entire video is obtained through the prediction function H. In the literature [14], G is implemented by taking the mean of the probability of all segment gesture categories, and H is implemented by the cross-entropy function. The process is shown in the following formula:

$$TSN(T_1, T_2, \cdots, T_K) = H(G(F(T_1; W), F(T_2; W), \cdots, F(T_K; W)))$$

$$(4.12)$$

where $F(T_k, W)$ represents the prediction result given by the convolutional network with W as the parameter when the input is T_k.

4.3 Basic operations of 3D convolutional neural network

In the previous sections, we introduced the basic operations of CNN and the application of CNN in gesture recognition. It is evident that CNNs, due to their 2D nature involving convolution and pooling operations, are primarily suited for spatial feature modeling. To process video sequence data, which requires capturing temporal changes, techniques such as optical flow are necessary. However, the integrity of temporal information is limited by the performance of optical flow data extraction algorithms.

Therefore, to better model temporal information, researchers have introduced three-dimensional convolution and three-dimensional pooling operations and have proposed a three-dimensional CNN (3D CNN).

4.3.1 3D convolution

3D convolution performs convolution operations in three-dimensional space, with both its input and output being three-dimensional tensors. The mathematical model is expressed as follows:

$$S_{mnl} = 3DConv(x) = \sum_{i=1}^{I}\sum_{j=1}^{J}\sum_{k=1}^{K} w_{ijk}x_{m+i,n+j,l+k} + b, (1 \leq m \leq M, 1 \leq n \leq N, 1 \leq l \leq L)$$

(4.13)

Where S_{mnl} indicates the pixel value at coordinate indices m, n, and l in three dimensions of the output feature map; w_{ijk} indicates the value of the convolution kernel at coordinate indices I, j, and k in three dimensions; $x_{m+i,n+j,l+k}$ indicates the input pixel value corresponding to pixel S_{mnl}, I, J, and K, respectively, indicate the value range of the convolution kernel in three dimensions; b is the bias term corresponding to this layer; M, N, and L, respectively, indicate the value range of the output feature map in three dimensions. The comparison between 3D convolution and 2D convolution is shown in Fig. 4.8.

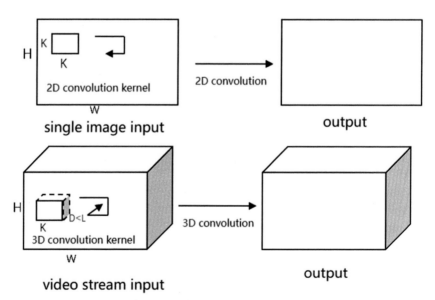

Figure 4.8 Comparison of 2D convolution and 3D convolution operations.

4.3.2 3D pooling

Similar to 3D convolution, 3D pooling is an extension of 2D pooling in the time dimension. The mathematical formula for a nonoverlapping max pooling operation with a pooling region size of $k_H \times k_W \times k_T$ is as follows:

$$o_{ijk} = 3DMAXPOOL(x) = \max_{m=1,2,\ldots,k_H} \max_{n=1,2,\ldots,k_W} \max_{l=1,2,\ldots,k_T} x_{s_H \times i+m, s_W \times j+n, s_T \times k+l}$$

(4.14)

Where o_{ijk} is the pixel value of the output feature map from max pooling at 3D coordinates I, j, and k, respectively; x is the input feature map to the pooling operation; k_H, k_W, and k_T are the value ranges of the pooling region in three dimensions; m, n, and l are the positional indices of the pixels participating in pooling within x, with value ranges of 1, 2, . . ., k_H, 1, 2, . . ., k_W, and 1, 2, . . ., k_T; s_H, s_W and s_T are the moving strides in the vertical and horizontal directions, respectively.

4.4 Application of 3D convolutional neural network in gesture recognition

Since gesture recognition tasks mostly require the recognition of a series of continuous actions rather than a single static image, many researchers have attempted to use 3D CNN to extract spatiotemporal features from gesture video data. Ji et al. [15] first applied 3D CNN for gesture and action recognition tasks. This model extends CNN convolution operations to enable the convolution of 3D data. Tran et al. [16] proposed the C3D network, which implements 3D convolution and 3D pooling. This network can extract spatiotemporal features simultaneously and has received much attention from researchers. Many methods for processing video sequences are based on this network. This section uses the C3D network and its improved versions as examples to introduce the application of 3D CNN in the field of gesture recognition.

4.4.1 C3D network

The C3D network was proposed by Tran et al. [16] in 2015. The biggest highlight of this network is the use of 3D convolution and 3D pooling operations to replace the 2D convolution and 2D pooling operations in CNN. On the one hand, compared with 2D convolution and pooling operations, the use of 3D convolution and 3D pooling can simultaneously extract spatial and temporal features of video data, thereby better learning the changes in gesture actions; on the other hand, this network structure enables end-to-end training, reducing the difficulty of network training, and is therefore favored by researchers.

The overall structure of the C3D network is shown in Fig. 4.9. The entire network consists of eight convolution layers, five pooling layers, two fully connected layers, and one Softmax layer. The convolution kernel sizes of the convolution layers are all $3 \times 3 \times 3$ with a stride of $1 \times 1 \times 1$. Among the five pooling layers, except for the first pooling layer with a pooling size of $1 \times 2 \times 2$, the other four pooling layers have a pooling size of $2 \times 2 \times 2$. This is to retain as much temporal information as possible in the early layers of the network.

Researchers have also proposed some new gesture recognition methods by combining the C3D network with other neural networks. Molchanov et al. [17] combined a C3D network with a recurrent neural network to further enhance the network's ability to learn temporal information. Camgoz et al. [18] first used a segmentation method similar to that in [14] TSN to segment continuous gesture videos, fed these video clips into the C3D network for classification, and finally obtained the gesture recognition result for the entire video through two-stage majority filtering.

Based on the C3D network, we have also carried out extensive research on large-scale gesture recognition problems and won the championship in the Chalearn LAP large-scale isolated gesture recognition challenge in both 2016 and 2017. In the 2016 competition, we proposed an RGB and depth data-based gesture recognition method [19] using the C3D network. This method uses a C3D network to extract spatiotemporal features from RGB video data and depth video data, fuses these two features through pointwise addition, and sends the fused features to a support vector machine (SVM) for classification, finally achieving an accuracy of 56.90% on the competition test set. Based on this, we studied the impact of different modal data on improving the performance of gesture recognition algorithms. We highlighted the performer's spatial position using generated saliency data, improving recognition accuracy to 59.43% [20]. We incorporated optical

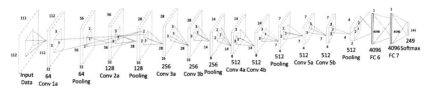

Figure 4.9 C3D network architecture.

flow data to highlight motion areas closely related to gestures and reduce the impact of irrelevant factors such as background, further improving gesture recognition accuracy to 60.93% [21].

Here we will elaborate on our method [19] used in the 2016 Chalearn LAP large-scale isolated gesture recognition challenge. The overall process is shown in Fig. 4.10. When analyzing the error results of using the original C3D network for gesture recognition, we find that since the network first performs temporal sampling on the input video to obtain a unified 16-frame video, some motion details may be lost for some longer videos, resulting in incorrect gesture classification by the network and affecting recognition accuracy. By analyzing the frame counts of all training videos in the CGD 2016 IsoGD dataset, which is a competition dataset, we find that most videos have between 29 and 39 frames, with videos consisting of 33 frames being the most common, totaling 1,202. Based on this finding, we respecify the temporal sampling frequency. To facilitate convolution and pooling operations in the time domain, we chose 32 frames as the reference for frame number normalization of all videos. In practice, we perform random sampling for videos with more than 32 frames and frame interpolation by replicating some frames for videos with less than 32 frames to expand the frame number. This processing method can ensure that more than 98% of videos can meet the requirement of at least one frame sampled every three frames, thus ensuring that the network can learn sufficient temporal information for the vast majority of videos.

In addition, since the CGD 2016 IsoGD dataset contains both RGB data and depth data, we also studied the methods to improve recognition accuracy by fusing multimodal data. As mentioned earlier, we extracted features of RGB data and depth data using the C3D model, combined the two modal features through pointwise addition fusion, and finally

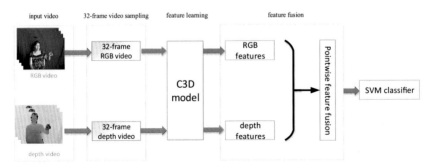

Figure 4.10 Large-scale gesture recognition algorithm based on C3D network [19].

performed gesture recognition using the fused features with an SVM classifier. Compared with using only RGB data or only depth data for gesture recognition, using fused features can improve accuracy by over 13%.

4.4.2 ResC3D network

In the previous section we introduced the advantages of the C3D network in simultaneously extracting spatiotemporal features from video data. However, as the number of layers increases, networks become difficult to optimize, and their performance may even deteriorate. To solve this problem, Tran et al. combined the residual network (ResNet) [22] with the C3D network and proposed the ResC3D network [9], further improving the performance of deep 3D CNN [23].

As mentioned above, the proposal of ResNet [22] was to solve the problem of difficulty in optimizing deep networks. The core of this network is the residual block. As shown in Fig. 4.11, in a residual block, x represents the feature input from the previous layer; $F(x)$ represents the result after two convolutions of the residual block, that is, $F(x) = W_2\sigma(W_1x)$, where W_1 and W_2 represent the weights of the first and second convolution layers, respectively (biases are omitted for simplicity); σ represents the ReLU activation function. In addition to these convolution layers, ResNet also adds a shortcut connection structure (the direct connection from x to "$\oplus$" in the figure on the right), which adds an identity mapping of the original input to the convolution result. It can be seen that when there is no identity mapping, the residual unit degenerates into an ordinary two-layer convolutional network. It is through this shortcut structure that ResNet can directly pass the original input information to

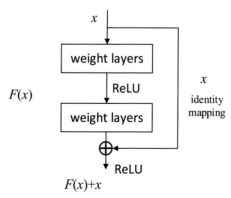

Figure 4.11 Residual unit architecture [22].

deeper convolution layers of the network, avoiding the problem of losing original input information due to multiple convolutions.

The overall structure of the ResC3D network is shown in Fig. 4.12. The network consists of eight residual units, corresponding to the eight convolution layers in the C3D model. Unlike the C3D network, the pooling layers are replaced by convolution layers with a stride of two, that is, downsampling is performed directly in the convolution layers conv3a, conv4a, conv5a, etc. Finally, the network uses an $7 \times 7 \times 1$ average pooling layer to reduce the dimensionality of the features for gesture recognition.

Researchers have also proposed many gesture recognition methods based on the ResC3D network. In the 2017 Chalearn LAP large-scale isolated gesture recognition challenge, we proposed a gesture recognition method [24] based on the ResC3D network. The framework is shown in Fig. 4.13. Noting the impact of irrelevant factors and noise on the recognition process, we first preprocess different modal data for data augmentation. For RGB data, the main interference comes from changes in illumination, so we eliminated the effect of illumination on RGB data using the Retinex algorithm. For depth data, the main interference is noise generated during imaging, so we denoised it using a median filter algorithm. Similar to our earlier research [21], this method also uses optical flow as an additional data modality for gesture recognition. Simultaneously, we found that various stages of a video differ in their significance for gesture recognition. The

Figure 4.12 ResC3D network architecture [24].

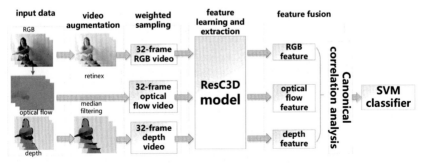

Figure 4.13 Large-scale gesture recognition algorithm based on ResC3D network [24].

actions are slower at the beginning and end of the video, while more intense during the climax, and more correlated with the gesture. Based on this finding, we proposed a weighted sampling method. This method uses optical flow data to determine the motion magnitude of the video at different stages and uses this as the basis for determining the proportion of frames sampled from each stage in the total sampled frames of the video. After sampling, the video data is fed into the ResC3D network for feature extraction. After using ResC3D for feature extraction on the three different modal data of RGB, optical flow, and depth, we analyzed the correlations between the features of different modalities using a feature fusion method based on canonical correlation analysis, and performed feature fusion accordingly. Similar to our earlier studies [19], the final recognition result was given by an SVM classifier. This method achieves an accuracy of 67.71% on the CGD 2016 IsoGD dataset.

4.4.3 Two-stream inflated 3D ConvNet (I3D) network

The two-stream inflated 3D ConvNet (I3D) [25] combines the advantages of 2D convolution and 3D convolution to achieve spatiotemporal feature learning. At the same time, this method also draws on the advantages of a two-stream network [13] by processing RGB data and optical flow data simultaneously. As shown in Fig. 4.14, the left branch of the network inputs RGB data into the 3D CNN to learn spatial domain features. The right branch inputs optical flow data into the 3D CNN to learn temporal domain features. Finally, the network fuses the extracted features from the two branches to generate the final recognition result.

Based on the I3D network structure, Wang et al. proposed a radar-based hand gesture recognition method [26] using time-sequential inflated three-dimensional convolution (TS-I3D). As shown in Fig. 4.15, Wang et al. first obtained gesture data using a frequency-modulated continuous wave radar sensor and converted it into range-Doppler images (RDM). After obtaining the range-Doppler image mapping of continuous gestures, Wang et al. fed it into the I3D network for feature extraction. Then, according to the data structure characteristics, the extracted features are reorganized into range-time and Doppler-time feature sequences, and the generated feature sequences are input into LSTM networks for further temporal feature extraction.

The I3D network structure used in this method is shown in Fig. 4.16. The input data size of the network is $32 \times 32 \times 64$. Wang et al. first used

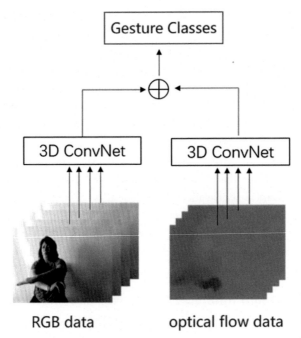

Figure 4.14 I3D network architecture [25].

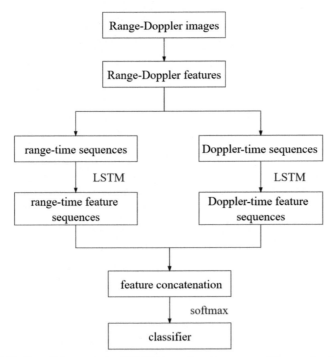

Figure 4.15 Overall framework of TS-I3D-based gesture recognition method [26].

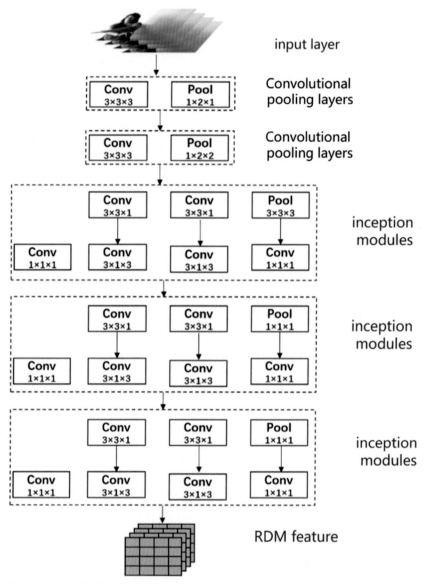

Figure 4.16 Radar-based gesture recognition network architecture using TS-I3D [26].

two modules composed of convolution layers and pooling layers to extract the shallow features in the RDM. Then Inception modules with convolution kernels of different receptive fields are used to further extract and integrate features to enhance feature richness.

4.5 Summary

With the development of deep CNN technology, researchers have made major breakthroughs in studying various problems in the field of computer vision. Compared with traditional methods, CNNs have not only greatly improved algorithm performance but also significantly reduced the difficulty of feature extraction. Researchers no longer need to design sophisticated features to obtain good results. This chapter first introduces the development history of CNN and then introduces the basic principles and operations of 2D CNN and 3D CNN, as well as their applications in gesture recognition tasks.

References

[1] D.H. Hubel, T.N. Wiesel, Receptive fields, binocular interaction and functional architecture in the cat's visual cortex, The Journal of Physiology 160 (1) (1962) 106–154.
[2] K. Fukushima, S. Miyake, Neocognitron: a self-organizing neural network model for a mechanism of visual pattern recognition, Competition and Cooperation in Neural Nets, Springer, Berlin, Heidelberg, 1982, pp. 267–285.
[3] Y. LeCun, L. Bottou, Y. Bengio, et al., Gradient-based learning applied to document recognition, Proceedings of IEEE 86 (11) (1998) 2278–2324.
[4] A. Krizhevsky, I. Sutskever, G.E. Hinton, Imagenet classification with deep convolutional neural networks, Proceedings on Advances in Neural Information Processing Systems, 1097-11, 2012, p. 05.
[5] C. Szegedy, W. Liu, Y. Jia, et al., Going deeper with convolutions, Proceedings of IEEE Conference on Computer Vision and Pattern Recognition, 2015, pp. 1–9.
[6] K. He, X. Zhang, S. Ren, et al., Delving deep into rectifiers: surpassing human-level performance on imagenet classification, Proceedings of IEEE International Conference on Computer Vision, 2015, pp. 1026–1034.
[7] K. Chen, J. Pang, J. Wang, et al., Hybrid task cascade for instance segmentation, Proceedings of IEEE Conference on Computer Vision and Pattern Recognition, 2019, pp. 4974–4983.
[8] W. Li, Z. Wang, B. Yin, et al., Rethinking on multi-stage networks for human pose estimation, arXiv preprint arXiv 00148 (1901) 2019.
[9] L. Yang, Q. Song, Z. Wang, et al., Parsing R-CNN for instance-level human analysis, Proceedings of IEEE Conference on Computer Vision and Pattern Recognition, 2019, pp. 364–373.
[10] L. Bondi, L. Baroffio, M. Cesana, et al., Rate-energy-accuracy optimization of convolutional architectures for face recognition, Journal of Visual Communication and Image Representation 36 (2016) 142–148.
[11] V. Nair, G.E. Hinton, Rectified linear units improve restricted boltzmann machines, Proceedings of International Conference on Machine Learning, 2010, pp. 807–814.
[12] J. Nagi, F. Ducatelle, G.A. Di Caro, et al., Max-pooling convolutional neural networks for vision-based hand gesture recognition, Proceedings of IEEE International Conference on Signal and Image Processing Applications, IEEE, 2011, pp. 342–347.

[13] K. Simonyan, A. Zisserman, Two-stream convolutional networks for action recognition in videos, Proceedings on Advances in Neural Information Processing Systems, 2014, pp. 1–11.

[14] L. Wang, Y. Xiong, Z. Wang, et al., Temporal segment networks: towards good practices for deep action recognition, Proceedings of European Conference on Computer Vision, Springer, Cham, 2016, pp. 20–36.

[15] S. Ji, W. Xu, M. Yang, et al., 3D convolutional neural networks for human action recognition, IEEE Transactions on Pattern Analysis and Machine Intelligence 35 (1) (2012) 221–231.

[16] D. Tran, L. Bourdev, R. Fergus, et al., Learning spatiotemporal features with 3D convolutional networks, Proceedings of IEEE International Conference on Computer Vision, 2015, pp. 4489–4497.

[17] P. Molchanov, X. Yang, S. Gupta, et al., Online detection and classification of dynamic hand gestures with recurrent 3D convolutional neural network, Proceedings of IEEE Conference on Computer Vision and Pattern Recognition, 2016, pp. 4207–4215.

[18] N.C. Camgoz, S. Hadfield, O. Koller, et al., Using convolutional 3d neural networks for user-independent continuous gesture recognition, Proceedings of International Conference on Pattern Recognition, IEEE, 2016, pp. 49–54.

[19] Li Yunan, Miao Qiguang, Tian Kuan, et al., Large-scale gesture recognition with a fusion of RGB-D data based on the C3D model, Proceedings of International Conference on Pattern Recognition, IEEE, 2016, pp. 25–30.

[20] Y. Li, Q. Miao, K. Tian, et al., Large-scale gesture recognition with a fusion of RGB-D data based on saliency theory and C3D model, IEEE Transactions on Circuits and Systems for Video Technology 28 (10) (2018) 2956–2964.

[21] Y. Li, Q. Miao, K. Tian, et al., Large-scale gesture recognition with a fusion of RGB-D data based on optical flow and the C3D model, Pattern Recognition Letters 119 (2019) 187–194.

[22] K. He, X. Zhang, S. Ren, et al., Deep residual learning for image recognition, Proceedings of IEEE Conference on Computer Vision and Pattern Recognition, 2016, pp. 770–778.

[23] D. Tran, J. Ray, Z. Shou, et al., Convnet architecture search for spatiotemporal feature learning, arXiv preprint arXiv 05038 (1708) 2017.

[24] Q. Miao, Y. Li, W. Ouyang, et al., Multimodal gesture recognition based on the resc3d network, Proceedings of IEEE International Conference on Computer Vision Workshops, 2017, pp. 3047–3055.

[25] J. Carreira, A. Zisserman, Quo vadis, action recognition? a new model and the kinetics dataset, Proceedings of IEEE Conference on Computer Vision and Pattern Recognition, 2017, pp. 6299–6308.

[26] Y. Wang, S. Wang, M. Zhou, et al., TS-I3D based hand gesture recognition method with radar sensor, IEEE Access 7 (2019) 22902–22913.

CHAPTER 5

Enhancing gesture recognition with advanced recurrent neural networks and memory networks

The proposal of convolutional neural networks provides a new solution for extracting image features. However, convolutional neural networks (CNNs) primarily focus on hierarchical processing through layered connections, and there is no connection between different neurons in the same layer. Therefore, CNN cannot effectively extract the features of sequential data with temporal or spatial relationships, such as voice and video. To better process this type of sequential data, researchers have proposed recurrent neural networks (RNNs), which are specially designed to handle sequential data with dependencies over time or space. This chapter will start with the technical advancements of RNN, then introduce the application of RNN and its variants, such as long short-term memory (LSTM), in the field of gesture recognition, and finally analyze the role of external storage units in feature extraction of long sequence data using memory networks.

5.1 Overview of development of recurrent neural networks

In 1982, American physicist Hopfield proposed a single-layer feedback neural network called Hopfield Network [1] and applied it to solve combinatorial optimization problems. This single-layer feedback neural network is the prototype of the recurrent neural network. In 1986, Michael I. Jordan defined the concept of loops and proposed the Jordan Network [2]. In 1990, American cognitive scientist Jeffrey L. Elman improved the interlayer connection method of the Jordan Network and obtained an RNN model that included recurrent connections for each node, forming a structure to capture temporal sequences. The connection between each unit in the RNN model is simple, and the model loses the information learned by units far from the current unit during layer-by-layer iteration, making it unable to retain long-term memory information. In 1997, Hochreiter and Schmidhuber proposed the LSTM

Gesture Recognition
DOI: https://doi.org/10.1016/B978-0-443-28959-0.00002-9

network [3], which solved the problem of long-term memory through gating units. In 2014, Cho et al. proposed the gate recurrent unit (GRU) [4], which reduces one gating unit based on LSTM and reduces network parameters without changing functionality. Furthermore, traditional RNN models typically only process inputs preceding the current time step, but the sequence data is interrelated, so the model may not be able to fully learn this sequence relationship. Therefore, in 1997, Mike Schuster proposed the bidirectional RNN model [5], which learns the contextual information of input sequences through two information flows passing in opposite directions. These models extend the application scenarios of RNN and lay a solid foundation for the development of subsequent serialization modeling. Afterward, many researchers improved the network's processing ability for long sequence data by adding auxiliary structures to RNN or directly introducing external memory units.

5.2 Recurrent neural networks and their variants

5.2.1 Basic structure of recurrent neural networks

The basic structure of RNN is relatively simple. Compared with general CNN networks, RNNs add a linear structure between equal levels, allowing information flow to be transmitted unidirectionally between nodes in each layer. Each node consists of an input layer, a hidden layer, and an output layer, as shown in Fig. 5.1.

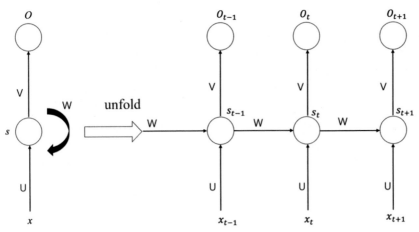

Figure 5.1 Basic structure diagram of RNN.

Where x_t represents the input received by the network at time t; s_t is the hidden layer state at time t, which is calculated from the input x_t at the current time and the hidden layer state s_{t-1} at the previous time. This process is the core of RNN implementation for memorizing previous inputs; and o_t is the output value at time t. The definitions of s_t and o_t are as follows:

$$s_t = f(Ux_t + Ws_{t-1}) \tag{5.1}$$

$$o_t = g(Vs_t) \tag{5.2}$$

Among them, U, V, W are weight matrices and $f(\cdot)$ and $g(\cdot)$ are activation functions. It can be seen that the output at each moment in RNN is affected by the hidden layer state of the previous moment. In theory, s_t should include the hidden layer state at time $1, 2, \ldots, t-1$; however, in practice, due to network structure and size limitations of s_t, it is likely that s_t only contains a small number of hidden layer states at the previous time rather than at all times.

5.2.2 Bidirectional recurrent neural networks

In RNN, information flows in only one direction, where the network only considers information before the current moment and does not consider information after the current moment. However, in many scenarios, the preceding and following contents of sequential data are related to each other, and the one-way characteristics of traditional RNNs make the network unable to learn the important information after the current moment, which leads to the prediction results not being accurate enough. For example, in the sentence: "Xiao Ming plays football," when it is necessary to predict the word "plays," it cannot be accurately predicted solely from the previous text "Xiao Ming." However, when combined with the text "football," it is easy to predict that the corresponding word should be "kick." Bidirectional RNN is also based on the idea of learning the contextual information of input sequences and making predictions through two information flows passing in opposite directions. These two information flows are called hidden states, with one passing in positive order, as shown by the solid line in Fig. 5.2. The other is transmitted in reverse order, as shown by the dashed line in Fig. 5.2.

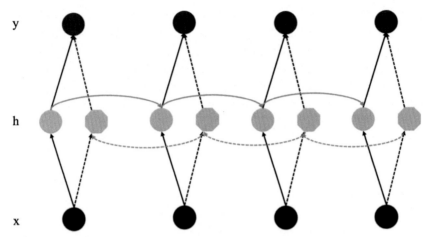

y

h

x

Figure 5.2 Bidirectional RNN network structure.

When calculating the hidden layer state at time t, for the positive sequence information flow, the input of the hidden layer state is the current time input, and for the previous positive order hidden layer state, or the reverse order information flow, the input is the input at the current time and the state of the reverse order hidden layer at the next time. Specifically, the positive order hidden layer state $\vec{h}_t$ is defined as follows:

$$\vec{h}_t = f(\vec{W}x_t + \vec{V}\vec{h}_{t-1} + \vec{b}) \tag{5.3}$$

The reverse order hidden layer state $\overleftarrow{h}_t$ is defined as follows:

$$\overleftarrow{h}_t = f(\overleftarrow{W}x_t + \overleftarrow{V}\overleftarrow{h}_{t+1} + \overleftarrow{b}) \tag{5.4}$$

The definition of output y_t is as follows:

$$y_t = g(U[\vec{h}_t; \overleftarrow{h}_t] + c) \tag{5.5}$$

Where $\vec{W}$, $\vec{V}$, $\overleftarrow{W}$, $\overleftarrow{V}$, and U represent the weight matrix; $\vec{b}$, $\overleftarrow{b}$, and c are biases; f and g are activation functions; $[\vec{h}_t; \overleftarrow{h}_t]$ indicates the concatenation of the positive sequence hidden layer state and the reverse sequence hidden layer state.

Compared with unidirectional RNN, the unique bidirectional hidden layer design of bidirectional RNN enables the model to better learn the input contextual information. However, at the same time, bidirectional RNN needs to store weight matrices in both directions, resulting in a larger storage space than RNN.

5.2.3 Long short term memory

Although RNNs can establish a relationship between the current input and the previous input to a certain extent, it can be seen from the parameter updates and information flow transmission process of RNNs that they do not perform information filtering on hidden states, which can result in redundant information within the network. Taking video-based gesture recognition as an example, when the performer's action amplitude is small, the difference between the current frame and the previous frame's action is also small. In this case, the information contained in the previous frame may be invalid or redundant for recognition. Therefore, it may be necessary to contact earlier input information to help us learn about the current input. Since the basic RNN almost only retains the information of the previous node, RNN cannot solve the long-term dependency problem. To address this issue, Hochreiter and Schmidhuber proposed the LSTM network [3] in 1997. This network filters input information through a gate structure. A gate structure is a structure that selectively allows information to pass through, consisting of neural network layers and element product operations. As shown in Fig. 5.3, there are three different gate structures designed in LSTM: input gate, forget gate, and output gate. These three structures work together to selectively preserve the information of previous nodes. Therefore, compared with RNN, LSTM is able to learn long-distance dependencies.

Each LSTM node has three inputs, namely the network input x_t at the current time, the hidden layer state h_{t-1} of the previous unit, and the cell unit state c_{t-1} of the previous unit. The output is the cell unit state c_t of the current unit and the hidden layer state h_t of the current unit.

In the three-gate structure of LSTM, the function of the input gate is to determine how much information the input x_t of the network at the

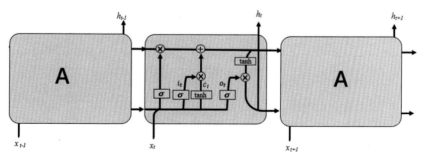

Figure 5.3 Long short-term memory basic unit.

current time is read into the cell state c_t of the current unit. As shown in Formula (5.6):

$$i_t = \delta(W_i[h_{t-1}, x_t] + b_i) \qquad (5.6)$$

W_i is the weight matrix of the input gate, and b_t is the bias term of the input gate.

The forget gate determines how much information in the cell state c_{t-1} of the previous unit is "forgotten" and retains the remaining portion of the current unit, similar to the process of the input gate. The process is shown in Formula (5.7):

$$f_t = \delta(W_f[h_{t-1}, x_t] + b_f) \qquad (5.7)$$

Where W_f is the weight matrix of the forgetting gate; b_f is the bias term of the forgetting gate; and δ is the sigmoid activation function.

After obtaining the input information at the current time through the input gate and selectively preserving the state information of previous nodes through the forgetting gate, the current cell state c_t can be represented by Formula (5.8):

$$c_t = f_t \cdot c_{t-1} + i_t \cdot a_t \qquad (5.8)$$

Where $a_t = \tanh(W_c \cdot [h_{t-1}, x_t] + b_c)$ represents the candidate cell state and b_c is the bias term.

Finally, the process of controlling how much information the current unit cell state c_t has to output to the current unit hidden layer state h_t is controlled by the output gate, which is defined as follows:

$$o_t = \tanh(W_o \cdot [h_{t-1}, x_t] + b_o) \qquad (5.9)$$

Where W_o is the weight matrix of the output gate; b_0 is the bias term; and the final output h_t can be expressed as:

$$h_t = o_t \cdot \tanh(c_t) \qquad (5.10)$$

The above is the structure of the entire LSTM. LSTM solves the problem of long-distance dependence by adding or removing information about the unit-cell state c_t through a gating mechanism.

5.2.4 Gate recurrent unit

LSTM solves the problem of long-distance dependency that traditional RNNs cannot solve. However, LSTM has the disadvantage of high computational complexity. Therefore, Cho et al. [5] proposed a new variant of LSTM, the GRU. GRU has a simpler structure than LSTM networks, thus reducing the number of parameters that the network needs to learn. In the GRU model, there are only two gate structures: the update gate and the reset gate. The update gate is formed by merging the input gate and the forgetting gate in LSTM. Fig. 5.4 shows the basic structure of GRU.

Where z_t and r_t represent update gates and reset gates, respectively; z_t is used to control the degree to which input information at the current time is written into the hidden layer state. The larger the value of z_t, the more input at the current time is written into the hidden layer state; r_t is used to control the degree to which the previous hidden layer state is written into the current hidden layer state h_t; and a smaller value of r_t indicates that the previous information is written less. The definition of update gate z_t is as follows:

$$z_t = \sigma(W_z \cdot [h_{t-1}, x_t]) \tag{5.11}$$

Where σ is the activation function, W_z is the update gate weight matrix, h_{t-1} is the hidden layer state at the previous time, and x_t is the current input matrix.

The definition of reset gate r_t is as follows:

$$r_t = \sigma(W_r \cdot [h_{t-1}, x_t]) \tag{5.12}$$

Where W_r is the reset gate weight matrix.

The hidden layer candidate state $\tilde{h}_t$ is defined as follows:

$$\tilde{h}_t = \tanh(W_h \cdot [h_{t-1}, r_t, x_t]) \tag{5.13}$$

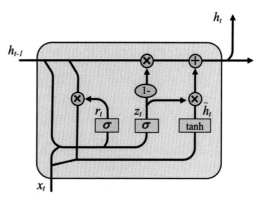

Figure 5.4 GRU network structure.

Where tanh($\cdot$) is the activation function. The current hidden layer state h_t is defined as follows:

$$h_t = (1 - z_t) \cdot h_{t-1} + z_t \tilde{h}_t \qquad (5.14)$$

Like LSTM, GRU also filters temporal features through a gate structure. However, since GRU reduces the number of parameters by one gate structure, compared with LSTM, it has a faster training speed. GRU may be a more suitable choice when considering the computing power and time cost of hardware.

5.3 Memory network combined with external storage units

5.3.1 Entropic associative memory and memory networks proposed by facebook AI research institute

LSTM and GRUs preserve historical input data through their internal memory cells, facilitating memory capabilities. Nevertheless, the training process for LSTMs and GRUs entails frequent updates to each memory cell, a procedure limited by the finite size of the cells and the constraints of the current hardware. To circumvent this limitation, memory networks that incorporate external storage units utilize selective read and write operations, allowing these networks to maintain information over extended periods. These networks achieve this by leveraging external storage, significantly expanding their memory capacity without necessitating updates to all cells concurrently. Pioneering research in this domain includes neural Turing machines (NTMs) by DeepMind [6] and Memory Networks by Facebook AI Research [7]. These advancements illustrate the potential for augmenting neural network memory for complex computational tasks.

5.3.2 Memory network framework

A memory network generally refers to a framework that remembers information by introducing an external memory unit. As illustrated in Fig. 5.5, the basic architecture of a memory network comprises four primary components that can be adapted for various tasks in practical applications. These are the input module (input feature map, I), generalization module (generalization, G), output module (output feature map, O), and conversion module (response, R) with the following functions:

I: Transforming the network input into feature vectors;

G: Updating the memory unit after the model has received input;

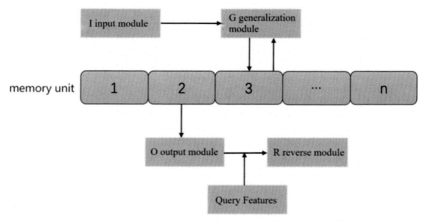

Figure 5.5 Memory network framework.

O: Integrating the similarity of memory units based on the input feature vector input from the network to obtain the output vector.

R: Converting the output vector into the target format, such as classifications for gesture recognition.

Among the four modules, *G* module and *O* module interact with the memory unit. *G* module is responsible for updating the memory unit, *O* module is responsible for reading data from the memory unit, and *I* module and *R* module serve as supporting modules for the memory network. The definition of the *G* module is as follows:

$$m_{H(x)} = I(x) \tag{5.15}$$

Where *x* represents network input, and *H(x)* is used to select the memory unit that needs to be updated, similar to the addressing operation in a computer. The *G* module only updates the memory units addressed by *H(x)*, while other memory units remain unchanged. The *O* module selects the first *k* most relevant memory units from all memory units based on the input feature vectors. The specific steps are as follows:

First, select the most relevant memory unit in memory:

$$m_{o1} = O_1(x, m) = \underset{S_0}{\operatorname{argmax}}(x, m_i) \tag{5.16}$$

Where S_0 is the similarity function that calculates the input vector and each memory unit. The range of values for *i* is 1 to *N*, where *N* is the size of the memory unit.

Then, combined with m_{o1} and input x, select the memory m_{o2} that is most relevant to them. Its definition is as follows:

$$m_{o2} = O_2([x, m_{o1}], m) = \underset{S_1}{\mathrm{argmax}}([x, m_{o1}], m_i) \qquad (5.17)$$

Repeat the above steps and obtain m_{o_k} through s_0 and $\{m_{o_1}, m_{o_2}, \ldots, m_{o_{k-1}}\}$ operations, thereby selecting the k memory units with the most similar input among all memory units. Subsequently, transfer the obtained x and the most similar k memory units $m_{o_1}, m_{o_2}, \ldots, m_{o_k}$ to the R module and use them to obtain the final result. The definition of R module is as follows

$$r = \underset{S_R}{\mathrm{argmax}}([x, m_{o1}, m_{o2}, \ldots, m_{ok}], w) \qquad (5.18)$$

A memory network is a universal framework. Based on memory networks, researchers have proposed further improvements, such as end-to-end memory networks [8] and dynamic memory networks [9].

5.3.3 Neural turing machine

The NTM refers to the Turing machine in computer architecture, which consists of a controller and a memory matrix, as shown in Fig. 5.6. If we compare a NTM with a computer, the controller is the CPU, and the memory matrix is the register. The controller performs read and write operations on the memory matrix based on input, thereby continuously

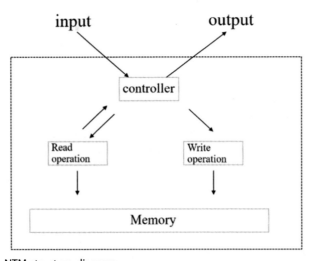

Figure 5.6 NTM structure diagram.

updating the memory unit. In the specific implementation process, the controller can be implemented by a simple feedforward network, or RNN. The advantages of feedforward networks are low computational complexity and high transparency. The advantage of RNN is that it can expand the read and write scale through its own internal memory storage mechanism, so each time step is not limited by a single read and write. Therefore, the controllers of NTMs are mostly composed of RNNs or their variants.

The core of a NTM is reading and writing, and the two parts will be introduced separately.

5.3.3.1 Reading operation

The controller determines the memory size r_t read from the memory matrix through a read operation. The controller reads useful information from the memory matrix based on the current input. At time t, the memory matrix M_t is a matrix of $N \times M$; N is the capacity of the memory unit; M is an independent memory vector; and W_t is the weight vector of N memories at time t. At time t, the memory read is defined as follows:

$$r_t = \sum_i^N W_t(i) \cdot M_t(i) \tag{5.19}$$

where $\sum_i^N W_t(i) = 1$, its fundamental idea is a weighted summation performed on N memories.

5.3.3.2 Writing operation

Similar to the LSTM, the NTMs writing operation also involves gating mechanisms that select and regulate information flow but is adapted to NTM's unique architecture. First, how LSTM writes the information of the current moment to the hidden layer is reviewed. LSTM consists of three gating units, the input gate selects the information retained from the input, the forgetting gate selects the information discarded from the hidden layer, the updating gate adds the retained information and subtracts the discarded information, and finally writes the information of the current moment to the hidden layer.

Next, we will provide a detailed introduction to the writing operation of the NTM. First, using the information in the controller, generate an erase vector e_t and an add vector a_t which respectively represent the amount of information to be added and deleted. The size of each element in the vector is 0 to 1, and the length of the vector is N. Then, e_t is used to perform an erase operation, and the extent of erasure is determined by the weight w_t, which is defined as follows:

$$M'_t(i) = M_{t-1}(i)[1 - w_t(i)e_t(i)] \qquad (5.20)$$

The above operation means erasing some information from the memory at time $t-1$. If both w_t and e_t are 0, it indicates that no erasure is needed. After performing the erasing operation, further writing operations is performed, which is defined as follows:

$$M_t(i) = M'_t(i) + w_t(i)a_t \qquad (5.21)$$

where a_t represents the newly written content of the memory unit by the controller. $w_t(i)$ represents the weight written to the i memory unit, and directly determines the correlation between the current input and memory. Two mechanisms have been proposed in NTMs to determine w_t, namely content-based addressing and location-based addressing.

5.3.3.2.1 Content-based addressing mechanism

The content-based addressing mechanism uses the cosine similarity function for addressing. This mechanism first takes the k_t vector provided by the controller as the query vector, then calculates the cosine similarity with k_t and each memory unit in M_t, and normalizes these values through the Softmax function to obtain the weight w_t^c based on the content addressing mechanism, which is as follows:

$$w_t^c = \frac{\exp(\beta_t K[k_t, M_t(i)])}{\sum_j \exp(\beta_t K[k_t, M_t(i)])} \qquad (5.22)$$

where $k[\cdot, \cdot]$ is the calculation of cosine similarity, defined as follows:

$$k[u, v] = \frac{u \cdot v}{\|u\| \cdot \|v\|} \qquad (5.23)$$

5.3.3.2.2 Location-based addressing mechanism

Location-based addressing mechanisms mainly consider the positional relationships of different memory units to design weights. This addressing mechanism can be divided into three steps:

5.3.3.2.2.1 Interpolation

Interpolation is a linear combination of weights. Based on obtaining the content-based addressing weight w_t^c, the threshold g_t is first designed to linearly combine the weight w_{t-1}^c of the previous time step $t - 1$ with the weight w_t^c of the current time step t to obtain a new weight w_t^g:

$$w_t^g = g_t w_t^c + (1 - g_t) w_{t-1}^c \tag{5.24}$$

5.3.3.2.2.2 Shift For each position element $w_t^g(i)$ in w_t^g, consider its adjacent k position elements, and consider these k elements to be related to $w_t^g(i)$. For example, when $k = 3$, the three adjacent elements are $w_t^g(i)$ itself, the element $w_t^g(i - 1)$, which is one position away and the element $w_t^g(i + 1)$, which is also one position away. A length-3 offset weight vector s_i is used to represent the weights of these three elements. Then the weighted sum is calculated to obtain the output value w_t, which can be specifically expressed as follows:

$$w_t' = \sum_{j=0}^{N} w_t^g(i + j) s(j) \tag{5.25}$$

The sum of all elements in the offset vector is 1, and the specific value of each element is a hyperparameter, which can be designed according to needs. For example, for the case where $k = 3$ mentioned above, a feasible offset vector is $[0.1, 0.8, 0.1]$.

5.3.3.2.2.3 Sharpen Although the offset operation can consider the influence of other memory units in the memory network on weights, excessive consideration can cause weights to be evenly distributed across all memory units, thereby reducing the impact of memory units on the results. Therefore, NTM designs sharpening operations to enhance the network's attention to target memory units. Specifically, the controller generates a parameter $\gamma_t > 1$ and normalizes each weight value with γ_t, as follows:

$$w_t(i) = \frac{w_t'(i)^{\gamma_t}}{\sum_j w_t'(i)^{\gamma_t}} \tag{5.26}$$

Finally, we obtain the final $w_t(i)$ for extracting and storing memories.

The entire NTM structure consists of two parts: a controller and a memory matrix. The controller is the core of the entire NTM, and the reading and writing operations of the memory matrix require the controller to generate various weights for auxiliary calculations. The reading operation is responsible for reading the required memory from the memory matrix, while the writing operation erases and writes to the memory matrix based on the erase vectors and add vectors generated by the controller. After a round of reading and writing operations, the controller once again obtains the final output of the model based on the information returned by the reading operation.

5.4 Application of recurrent neural network in gesture recognition

Image-based gestures are composed of a single image, while video-based gestures are composed of videos or consecutive images. The input data in video-based gesture recognition is a type of serialized data that cannot be replaced by a particular frame or frames. When conducting gesture recognition, it is necessary to consider the contextual relationship of input data, so the modeling method of image-based gestures is not applicable to continuous gestures. Traditional two-dimensional neural networks are mainly used to extract spatial information from data, but it is difficult to extract temporal information from input data using this method. Therefore, in video-based gesture recognition, network structures such as recurrent neural networks or memory networks that can effectively extract temporal information are used for recognition. First, convolutional networks are used to extract spatial information from input data, and then recurrent neural networks or memory networks are used to process temporal information to solve the problem of video-based gesture recognition.

5.4.1 Application of recurrent neural networks in gesture recognition

The difficulty of video-based gesture recognition in real-world human-computer interaction scenarios lies in how to provide real-time feedback on recognition results to users. To provide users with fast feedback in video-based gesture recognition, Molchanov et al. [10] proposed a video-based gesture recognition algorithm that utilizes three-dimensional convolutional neural networks (3DCNNs) and RNNs. As shown in Fig. 5.7, input video is divided into N segments, each with m frames (where $m \geq 1$). Feed each video segment into a 3DCNN to extract the spatiotemporal features $f_t, f_{t+1}, \ldots, f_{t+N}$ of each video segment. Compared with sending the entire video into a 3DCNN to extract spatiotemporal features, the time required to extract spatiotemporal features separately after dividing the video into N segments is reduced by $1/N$, However, dividing consecutive videos into N segments disrupts temporal information, so RNN is introduced to extract

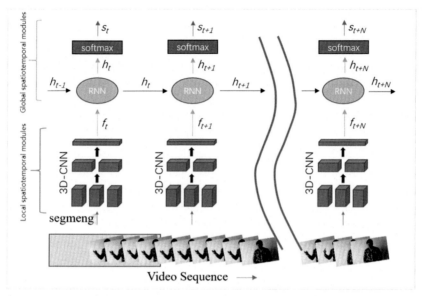

Figure 5.7 3D CNN and RNN video-based gesture recognition network [10].

the temporal information of the entire video by incorporating the spatio-temporal features of each segment obtained from a 3DCNN into RNN. RNN plays a role in integrating N video segments, filling in the time information lost due to video segmentation. Finally, the Softmax function is used to convert the hidden layer states $h_t, h_{t+1} \ldots h_{t+N}$ generated by RNN into N gesture probability values $s_t, s_{t+1} \ldots s_{t+N}$.

RNN can play a role in extracting temporal information in video-based gesture recognition. The input of video-based gesture recognition is serialized information, which is very consistent with the structure of RNN. Therefore, more and more research results have emerged that combine RNN and CNN for gesture recognition. Hu et al. [11] combined CNN with RNN and introduced attention mechanisms to explore temporal information between frames at a deeper level.

5.4.2 Application of long short term memory in gesture recognition

LSTM also has many applications in gesture recognition tasks. Zhu et al. used ConvLSTM combined with CNN for video-based gesture recognition. The essence of ConvLSTM is the same as LSTM, which takes the output of the previous layer as the input of the next layer. The difference is that ConvLSTM transforms all multiplication operations in LSTM into convolution operations. ConvLSTM can better combine temporal and spatial features, and ConvLSTM sets the step size of convolution operations to (1,1), which does not change the size of the spatial domain and does not cause loss of spatial information. The two-dimensional spatiotemporal features outputted at each time step integrate the spatiotemporal features of past frames, enabling a closer integration of spatiotemporal learning.

In 2017, Zhu et al. proposed an application that combines 3DCNN with ConvLSTM [12]. The structure is shown in Fig. 5.8. First, the input video is divided into several small video segments, and short-term spatiotemporal features are extracted using 3DCNN. Afterward, ConvLSTM is used to further learn the overall long-term characteristics. At the same time, to enable the network to better classify the output of ConvLSTM, they used spatial pyramid pooling to normalize the features, ensuring that videos of different lengths can have the same length of features and ultimately use this feature to complete classification.

In 2018, Zhu et al. [13] proposed a more effective network structure combining 3DCNN with ConvLSTM and applied it to continuous gesture recognition tasks. The network structure is shown in Fig. 5.9. First, a time-domain cavity Res3D network is used to segment continuous gesture sequences into independent gesture fragments. Considering the uneven number of boundary frames (transition frames between two gestures) and gesture frames, they used a balanced squared hinge loss function

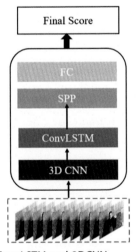

Figure 5.8 Combination of ConvLSTM and 3DCNN.

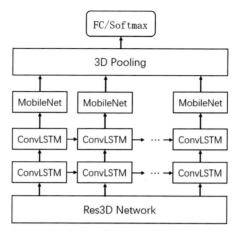

Figure 5.9 Combination of 3D CNN and ConvLSTM [13].

to address this issue. Finally, using a method similar to literature [12], they combined 3DCNN and ConvLSTM to extract long-term information between independent gestures and constructed a recognition network using 2DMobileNet to achieve the final recognition.

5.4.3 Application of combining memory network and long short term memory in gesture recognition

This section will introduce a gesture recognition algorithm proposed by Yuan et al. [14] that combines memory networks and LSTM. It decomposes the feature extraction process of gesture videos into two parts, time and space, and finally performs fusion. The network structure is shown in Fig. 5.10. The RGB branch is used to extract spatial information in videos, while the optical flow branch is used to extract temporal information in videos. The dual stream network structure can more intuitively extract the spatial and temporal information of videos.

First, CNNs are used to extract the features of RGB data and optical flow data, and then LSTM is used to obtain the contextual relationships of these features. At the same time, the memory controller is used to process the features at the current moment, and the eligible features are written into the memory to increase the "memory space." Finally, all the features in memory are merged to represent the input video, and the classification is performed using Softmax. The classification results are averaged by RGB or optical flow results.

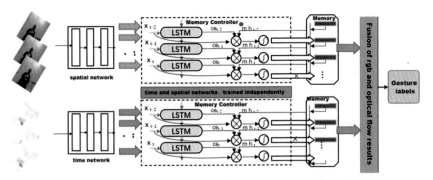

Figure 5.10 Structure diagram of memory network combined with LSTM. *Copyright ©*
2024, Association for the Advancement of Artificial Intelligence. Citation to the original
publication is required. All rights reserved should appear beneath figures, and permission
to reuse figures for other purposes (or granting it to others) is NOT allowed.

In this model, the read operation is to average all items in the memory
module at each time, defined as follows:

$$mh_t = \sum_{i=1}^{N_t} m_i \qquad (5.27)$$

where m_i represents the i block of memory in the memory module and
N_t represents the size of memory at the current time.

The write-operation is determined by the hidden layer state h_t output
by LSTM, the feature vector x_t of the current frame, and the feature vector mh_t read from memory at the current time to jointly determine
whether the feature vector of the current frame is written to memory.
The specific operation is as follows:

$$q_t = \sigma\left(v_s^T \cdot \text{ReLU}\left(W_{sf}x_t + W_{sh}h_t + W_{sm}mh_t + b_s\right)\right) \qquad (5.28)$$

where, W_{sf}, W_{sh}, W_{sm} represent the weight matrix and b_s is the deviation.
v_s^T is a variation matrix whose purpose is to transform the matrix after
passing through the ReLU function into a predicted value. σ represents
the sigmoid function. If the final q_t is greater than 0.5, x_t will be written
to memory, otherwise it will not be written to memory.

This algorithm cleverly combines LSTM and memory network to
solve the problem of limited memory of LSTM, while using a dual-
stream network to more fully utilize spatiotemporal information.

5.5 Summary

This chapter first introduces the recurrent neural network RNN and its variants, including LSTM, GRU, etc., as well as memory networks combined with external storage units. Subsequently, examples are provided to illustrate the application of different networks in the field of gesture recognition. It is worth noting that in gesture recognition, recurrent neural networks and memory networks generally only serve to extract time-domain information, so they are often used in conjunction with CNNs.

References

[1] J. Hopfield, Neural networks and physical systems with emergent collective computational abilities, Proceedings of National Academy of Sciences 79 (8) (1982) 2554−2558.

[2] M.I. Jordan, Serial order: a parallel distributed processing approach, Advances in Connectionist Theory (1989) 1−46.

[3] S. Hochreiter, J. Schmidhuber, Long short-term memory, Neural Computation 9 (8) (1997) 1735−1780.

[4] K. Cho, B. Van Merriënboer, C. Gulcehre, et al. Learning phrase representations using RNN encoder-decoder for statistical machine translation, in: Proceedings of Conference on Empirical Methods in Natural Language Processing, 2014, pp. 1−15.

[5] M. Schuster, K. Paliwal, Bidirectional recurrent neural networks, IEEE Transactions on Signal Processing 45 (11) (1997) 2673−2681.

[6] A. Graves, G. Wayne, I. Danihelka, Neural turing machines, arXiv preprint arXiv 1410 (2014) 5401.

[7] J. Weston, S. Chopra, A. Bordes, Memory networks, arXiv preprint arXiv 1410 (2014) 3916.

[8] S. Sukhbaatar, A. Szlam, J. Weston, et al., End-to-end memory networks, in: Proceedings on Advances in Neural Information Processing Systems, 2015, pp. 1−9.

[9] A. Kumar, O. Irsoy, P. Ondruska, et al. Ask me anything: dynamic memory networks for natural language processing, in: Proceedings of International Conference on Machine Learning, 2016, pp. 1378−1387.

[10] P. Molchanov, X. Yang, S. Gupta, et al. Online detection and classification of dynamic hand gestures with recurrent 3D convolutional neural network, in: Proceedings of IEEE Conference on Computer Vision and Pattern Recognition, 2016, pp. 4207−4215.

[11] Y. Hu, Y. Wong, W. Wei, et al., A novel attention-based hybrid CNN-RNN architecture for sEMG-based gesture recognition, PloS One 13 (10) (2018) e0206049.

[12] G. Zhu, L. Zhang, P. Shen, et al., Multimodal gesture recognition using 3-D convolution and convolutional LSTM, IEEE Access 5 (2017) 4517−4524.

[13] G. Zhu, L. Zhang, P. Shen, et al., Continuous gesture segmentation and recognition using 3DCNN and convolutional LSTM, IEEE Transactions on Multimedia 21 (4) (2018) 1011−1021.

[14] Y. Yuan, D. Wang, Q. Wang, Memory-augmented temporal dynamic learning for action recognition, in: Proceedings of AAAI Conference on Artificial Intelligence, 2019, pp. 9167−9175.

CHAPTER 6

Gesture recognition method based on multimodal data fusion

6.1 Techniques for acquiring multimodal data

6.1.1 Depth data

Depth images are commonly used as supplementary information in RGB computer vision tasks. The depth image reflects the distance of each point in the scene from the imaging device through different grayscale values of pixels. Therefore, depth data has been widely used in various computer vision tasks. Currently, methods for obtaining depth data can be divided into two categories based on the operating principle of filming equipment, namely passive sensors and active sensors. These two types of methods will be introduced separately below.

6.1.1.1 Passive sensors

Passive sensors can complete acquisition without the signal from the imaging device itself. The most commonly employed method is binocular stereovision, which relies on disparity estimation. It uses two imaging devices placed in crossed positions to capture the same object from different angles, and then the pixels in the two images can be matched and corresponded through a stereo-matching algorithm to calculate the disparity information. Finally, the distance information of objects in the scene is estimated based on the corresponding camera position parameters and other information. Currently, some monocular depth estimation algorithms do not require multiple imaging devices but only need to use the brightness features, contrast features, and other information of a single RGB image to estimate the depth of the target scene [1,2].

6.1.1.2 Active sensors

Compared with passive sensor methods, active sensors require equipment to signal to complete the collection of depth information. This signal can be infrared pulses, lasers or structured light, etc. There are many types of acquisition equipment based on active sensors, mainly including time-of-flight (TOF) cameras, lidar, structured light-depth cameras, etc.

Gesture Recognition
DOI: https://doi.org/10.1016/B978-0-443-28959-0.00005-4

Figure 6.1 Kinect camera physical diagram.

The principle of the TOF camera to obtain depth images is that the camera gives continuous near-infrared pulses to the target scene and receives the reflected signal from the object. By comparing the time difference between the transmitted and received infrared pulse signals, we can calculate the distance of the object relative to the transmitter and finally obtain a depth image to complete the estimation of the depth of the scene.

Lidar ranging technology is similar to TOF, but it emits lasers instead of near-infrared pulses. When acquiring depth data, the lidar will emit a laser at certain intervals to scan the entire scene. Subsequently, by calculating the time difference between emitting the laser and receiving the reflected signal from each scene point, the distance between the object and the lidar can be calculated. Compared with TOF cameras, lidar has the advantage of wide range and high accuracy. Therefore, lidar is widely used in visual systems for outdoor three-dimensional (3D) space perception.

Similar to the aforementioned methods, the structured light depth camera generally projects structured light into the scene and receives the returned structured light when estimating depth. Since the pattern of structured light will be deformed when projected onto different objects, by analyzing the position and deformation of the structured light received by the camera, the depth information of objects at different locations can be estimated.

As shown in Fig. 6.1, Kinect[1] is a somatosensory device by Microsoft that can simultaneously acquire RGB and depth images. It is a representative device that acquires depth images based on structured light. The original intention of Microsoft to develop this device was to obtain information for some motion-sensor games on its Xbox game console. However, recently, Kinect has also many applications in computer vision research, such as 3D scene reconstruction and multimodal information fusion. The RGB image and corresponding depth image obtained through Kinect are shown in Fig. 6.2.

---

[1] Detailed information can be found on the official website: https://developer.microsoft.com/windows/kinect/.

(A)   (B)

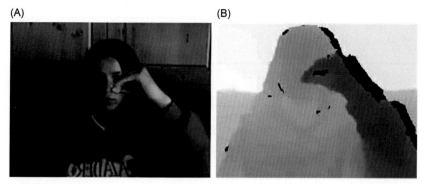

Figure 6.2 Visible light and depth image acquired by Kinect. (A) Kinect^2 captured visible light image of a person performing a gesture in an indoor setting. (B) Corresponding depth image showing shades of gray to represent object distances, highlighting the spatial contour and gesture of the person.

The development of the depth imaging equipment represented by Kinect has greatly improved the accessibility of depth data. Therefore, many researchers have begun to use depth data to research gesture recognition methods. For example, Dominio et al. [3] obtain gesture information from depth data only without calculating the complete pose in the entire image. Specifically, this method extracts the hand-corresponding area from the depth map and further subdivides it into palms and fingers. Then two sets of features can be extracted: one describing the distance from the fingertips to the center of the palm, and the other describing the curvature of the hand contour. Finally, a multiclass support vector machine (SVM) classifier is used to recognize different gestures.

6.1.2 Infrared data

Light is a kind of electromagnetic wave, ranging from gamma rays with wavelengths below the picometer level to radio waves with wavelengths of thousands of meters. Among them, the part visible to the human eye is called visible light. As shown in Fig. 6.3, the wavelength range of visible light is around 380–760 nm. The wavelength of infrared light is longer than that of red light, ranging from approximately 760 nm to 1 mm.

In nature, any object with a temperature above absolute zero (−273°C) emits infrared rays. This fundamental principle has led to the invention of infrared imaging technology. Infrared thermal imaging cameras are built

---

^{2} Data comes from Chalearn Large-scale Isolated Gesture Dataset.

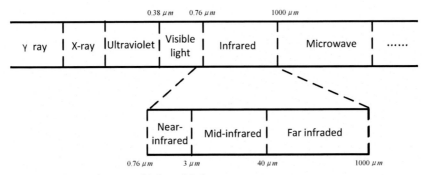

Figure 6.3 Spectral range of infrared light.

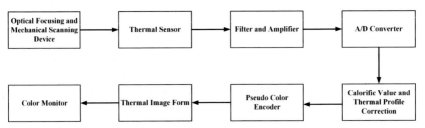

Figure 6.4 Working principles of thermal imager.

upon this principle and generate real-time infrared images by detecting the infrared radiation emitted by objects. During this process, the infrared thermal imaging device uses infrared sensors and ordinary optical imaging equipment to detect the infrared radiation signal of the target. After filtering and amplifying the detected signal, the optical signal is converted into an electrical signal through photoelectric conversion. Following various stages of processing and encoding, the data is transformed into a thermal image that can be visually displayed, ultimately appearing on the monitor. The workflow is illustrated in Fig. 6.4.

Infrared imaging can effectively represent information that is not visible in the visible light spectrum under low-light conditions more clearly. The image obtained through infrared imaging technology is shown in Fig. 6.5. It can be seen that there is an apparent difference between the human body and the background in the infrared image since the body heat is higher compared with the temperature of objects in the environment.

For gesture recognition tasks, Leite et al. [4] combine depth data and infrared data to achieve real-time static gesture recognition. This method utilizes depth maps for background removal and hand-position detection.

(A)   (B)

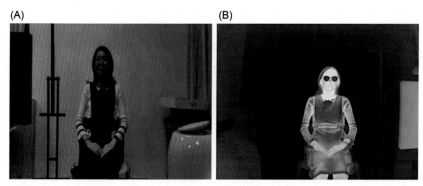

Figure 6.5 Visible light image and infrared image. (A) Visible light image of a person in a room. (B) Infrared image showing the heat signature of the same person and surroundings, with warmer areas appearing in brighter colors.

The hand position from the previous frame is then used for tracking to find the hand centroid for the current frame. The obtained centroid is used as the input of the region–growing algorithm, and the result of the algorithm is used to segment the hand area in the depth map. The segmentation result is applied to the infrared frame in the form of a mask. Each frame is then labeled as gesture or nongesture using motion constraints for gesture recognition. Frames marked as gestures are then enhanced through methods such as mask subtraction, contrast stretching, median filtering, and histogram equalization. Finally, SIFT features [5] are extracted from the enhanced gesture frames to construct a bag of visual words and classified through a multiclass SVM classifier.

Mantecón et al. [6] propose a real-time gesture recognition system based on near-infrared images, which are used to recognize static and dynamic gestures. The method consists of three main steps. Initially, it identifies the hand region by generating various candidate regions and assessing them with feature vectors. The most likely candidate is then selected based on confidence scores to pinpoint the hand's location. Subsequently, the identified hand regions across frames are analyzed for gesture classification. Finally, a voting mechanism consolidates these per-frame predictions into a feature vector, encapsulating the gesture sequence, which is then inputted into a SVM for the final gesture recognition.

6.1.3 Skeleton data

Skeleton data is used to record the location information of keypoints in the human body. It plays an important role in the tasks of pose estimation and action recognition. Therefore, the generation of skeleton data is the basis for many computer vision tasks, such as action recognition and posture estimation. The generation of skeleton data requires detecting some keypoints of the human body, such as the trunk, hands, elbows, knees, feet, etc. We abstract these keypoints as representations of human body information. By identifying and connecting these keypoints in accordance with the human body structure, a skeletal framework is constructed. In real life, the acquisition of skeleton data can be divided into the following three categories according to the imaging method or data acquisition source.

6.1.3.1 Using wearable sensor systems

A representative wearable device for acquiring skeleton data is the MoCap (motion capture) [7] device. After the performer wears the sensing device, MoCap collects the movement information of keypoints on the performers who already have wearable devices. Each keypoint of the data obtained via MoCap is generally in 3D coordinates, and these coordinates can be converted into corresponding skeleton images through certain mapping and visualization.

6.1.3.2 Estimating through RGB-D camera

As mentioned above, the depth information of the scene can be obtained through technologies such as structured light. When a person moves, the distance between different parts of their body and the imaging device also changes. Combined with the RGB data obtained by ordinary cameras, it is possible to describe the outline of the human body and information about different parts of the body, such as the head, hands, feet, and trunk, in a more refined manner. With some computer vision algorithms, the movement of joint points can be recorded to form corresponding skeleton data [8]. Kinect, the aforementioned RGB-D camera, is a device that can be used to extract skeleton data in this way through its corresponding development tool kits. However, it is worth noting that these devices estimate skeleton data based on images. When part of the human body is obscured or the acquired depth information is missing, the 3D coordinate information of the skeleton points cannot be completely estimated. In other words, the skeleton information obtained through this method is not necessarily accurate.

6.1.3.3 Approximating only with RGB images

Although depth cameras are relatively inexpensive compared with wearable sensors, they are still not widely affordable compared with regular RGB cameras. Therefore, some researchers also study how to estimate skeleton keypoints through a single RGB image. This estimation can be based on either 2D (two-dimensional) [9] or 3D information [10]. Since the human body has a certain degree of flexibility, even for the same movement, different people may have different postures due to the different degrees of curvature of their body parts. In addition, the visibility of keypoints is easily affected by the surroundings, such as the performer's clothing, posture, visual angle, etc. External environmental factors, such as occlusion and lighting, can also affect the detection of keypoints. Therefore, the detection of human skeleton keypoints still poses significant challenges. Here is a simple introduction to two methods for keypoint detection, namely, image morphology and deep learning.

Traditional human skeleton keypoint detection algorithms are essentially based on certain geometric priors and are always implemented by template matching. The key is how to use the idea of template matching to represent the human body structure, including the structure of each part and the relationship between different parts. Ideally, the template can match different postures during the action to ensure that keypoints of the human body can be detected throughout the entire action sequence [11].

The refinement of the skeleton extraction method is based on image morphology [12]. As shown in Fig. 6.6, the original image is processed to a thin connected region with a pixel width based on certain criteria by refining the contours. Without altering the contour shape, the final skeleton data is obtained for feature extraction and target topological representation.

In recent years, with the rapid development of deep learning, many CNN-based human body keypoint detection algorithms have been proposed. These can be roughly divided according to their directions: topdown and bottomup.

The topdown keypoint detection algorithm mainly includes two steps: object (human) detection and skeleton keypoint detection. This involves initially detecting the entire human body region through object detection, followed by implementing skeleton keypoint detection based on this result. There are three issues to consider for skeleton keypoint detection algorithms. First, there is difficulty in detecting different keypoints of the human body. For instance, detecting keypoints in the limbs and body is noticeably

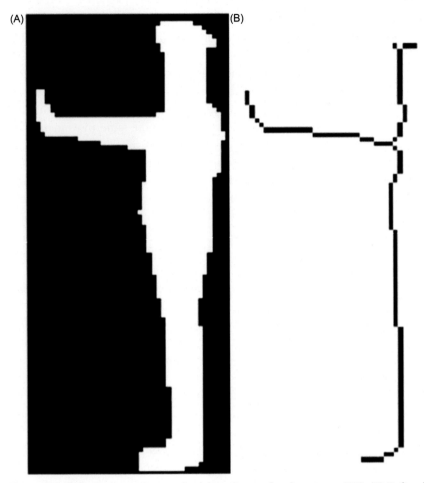

Figure 6.6 Skeleton extraction method based on refined contours [12]. (A) Refined contour representation of a shape. (B) Extracted skeletal structure from the contour.

more challenging than detecting keypoints in the head. Therefore, different keypoints may require distinct treatment. Second, the presence of similar local regions can make it difficult to detect keypoints. For example, if there are similar textures in the background and the clothing on the human body, it becomes difficult to separate the human body from the background. To address this issue, the use of a larger receptive field is often considered. Lastly, topdown keypoint localization relies on the detection boxes obtained from the object detection algorithm. Poor performance in the detection algorithm can lead to the occurrence of false positives.

The bottomup keypoint detection algorithm is mainly designed for multiperson skeleton keypoint detection. It mainly includes two steps: keypoint detection and keypoint clustering. The keypoint detection here is similar to that in the topdown method, and the only difference is that all keypoints should be detected first, even if they belong to different people in bottomup methods. Then a clustering algorithm is used to map these keypoints to different performers. This method focuses on how to better learn the differences between different keypoints of different people to achieve more accurate clustering.

OpenPose [13] is a deep neural network that detects keypoints of the human body. It employs multiple stages to learn human body postures. In the first stage it obtains heatmap predictions for different keypoints. In the subsequent stages, it iterates the predicted values of all heatmaps, optimizes the results of the previous stage, and infers the connection information between keypoints. The newly learned relationships between human body structures are then used to achieve final optimization, and the skeleton keypoint prediction results shown in Fig. 6.7 are finally obtained. The results of gesture keypoint prediction using OpenPose are shown in Fig. 6.8.

In addition to human body skeleton data, researchers have also conducted more research on hand skeleton data. To use complete 3D skeleton data to represent the shape of the hand, Smedt et al. [14] propose a new descriptor based on several related joint sets, namely shape of connected joints. This descriptor is encoded using Fisher vectors obtained

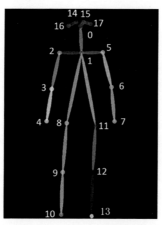

Figure 6.7 Example of skeleton keypoints extracted using OpenPose algorithm.

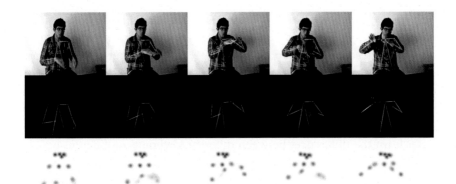

Figure 6.8 RGB data and comparison of skeleton maps and heatmaps extracted from it.

through the Gaussian mixture model. In addition, this method also utilizes skeleton data to extract hand orientation histogram features and wrist rotation histogram features and employs a temporal pyramid to extract temporal information about the entire hand motion. The final feature vector is classified using a linear SVM classifier.

Hou et al. [15] propose a spatiotemporal attention residual convolutional temporal network (STA-Res-TCN) based on skeleton data for dynamic gesture recognition. The network uses methods such as scaling, moving, temporal interpolation, and adding noise for data enhancement to prevent overfitting. STA-Res-TCN is then used for feature extraction and classification. The network adaptively learns different levels of attention through a mask branch based on temporal convolutional networks (TCNs) and integrates these attentions into the spatiotemporal features extracted by the backbone network. This attention branch can help the network adaptively focus on the temporal information of the sample while eliminating noise interference caused by irrelevant content.

In addition, some researchers use skeleton data together with other modal data. For example, Ioenescu et al. [16] propose a dynamic gesture recognition technology based on the 2D skeleton representation of the hand. This method superimposes the skeleton data of each gesture onto a single image generated as the dynamic feature of the gesture. Wang et al. [17] utilize depth maps and skeleton data provided by Kinect devices, employing the concept of superpixels to represent hand shapes and their corresponding textures. In addition, they also propose a distance measurement method called Superpixel Earth Mover's Distance to express the similarity between different gestures.

6.1.4 Optical flow data

In Section 3.2.6, we briefly introduce the definition of optical flow data. Generally speaking, optical flow is generated by the movement of objects in the scene, the movement of the camera, or the relative movement between the two. Optical flow primarily captures changes in images, and for gesture actions, which are inherently variations in a video sequence, optical flow data can be used to describe the motion of the hands.

In 1981, Horn et al. [18] linked optical flow to grayscale for the first time, introduced the optical flow constraint equation, and gave the basic method of optical flow calculation. Since then, researchers have begun to propose various optical flow calculation methods based on different theories. This section will introduce the method proposed by Brox et al. [19] to calculate optical flow characteristics through an energy equation based on brightness constancy, gradient constancy, and spatiotemporal smoothness constraint assumptions.

Before giving the above energy equation, the constraints required for the energy equation are discussed.

6.1.4.1 Brightness constancy assumption

Optical flow estimation generally assumes that the brightness value of a pixel is not affected by displacement:

$$I(x, y, t) = I(x + u, y + v, t + 1) \tag{6.1}$$

where $I: \Omega \subset R^3 \to R$ is a rectangular image sequence; $(u, v, 1)^{\mathrm{T}}$ is the search displacement vector between the image at step t and the image at step $t + 1$. By linearizing the brightness value constancy assumption, the famous optical flow constraint can be obtained, which can be expressed as:

$$I_x u + I_y v + I_t = 0 \tag{6.2}$$

where, let u and v represent the velocity vector of the optical flow along the axis x and axis y, respectively, and I represents the light intensity. This linearization only works if it is assumed that the image changes linearly along with the displacement.

6.1.4.2 Gradient constancy assumption

The assumption of brightness constancy has a big drawback. It is easily affected by brightness changes. In natural scenes, variations in brightness are quite common. Therefore, some small changes in brightness values need to be allowed. At the same time, a criterion that is not affected by changes in brightness values can be used to help determine the displacement vector, which is the gradient of the image brightness value. The gradient formula of the image brightness value is as follows:

$$\nabla I(x, y, t) = \nabla I(x + u, y + v, t + 1) \tag{6.3}$$

where $\nabla = (\partial_x, \partial_y)^T$ represents spatial gradient.

6.1.4.3 Spatiotemporal smoothness assumption

Under the above constraints, the model only estimates the displacement of a local pixel without considering the interaction between adjacent pixels. Therefore, once the gradient disappears somewhere or only the gradient in the normal direction can be estimated, the model will be wrong. In addition, some outliers may appear in the optical flow estimation. Therefore, it is necessary to introduce the smoothness assumption of the optical flow field. This smoothness constraint can be applied independently in the spatial domain when only two frames of images are available. Of course, it can also be applied to the spatiotemporal domain when it is necessary to calculate the displacement in an image sequence.

With the above assumptions and constraints, the energy equation used to calculate the optical flow characteristics can be given, as shown in Formula (6.4).

$$E(u, v) = E_{\text{Data}} + \alpha E_{\text{Smooth}} \tag{6.4}$$

where $\alpha > 0$ is a regularization parameter. E_{Data} can be expressed as:

$$E_{\text{data}}(u, v) = \int_{\Omega} \psi(|\Delta I(x)|^2) + \gamma |\Delta G(x)|^2 dx \tag{6.5}$$

where γ is the weight coefficient used to balance the two parts; ΔI and ΔG, respectively, represent the changes in brightness and gradient magnitude between two frames of the video; $\psi(s^2)$ is an increasing concave function used to enhance the robustness of the energy equation; Ω is the integration interval that represents the entire video and E_{Smooth} can be expressed as:

$$E_{\text{Smooth}}(u, v) = \int_{\Omega} \psi(|\nabla_3 u|^2 + |\nabla_3 v|^2) dx \tag{6.6}$$

where ∇_3 represents the spatiotemporal gradient in the smoothness constraint assumption. The final optical flow result is obtained by minimizing this energy function through the Lagrangian equation and numerical approximation. The optical flow data generated by this method is shown in Fig. 6.9.

Optical flow data is also a commonly used modal data in gesture recognition methods. Wang et al. [20] propose temporal segment networks

(A)   (B)

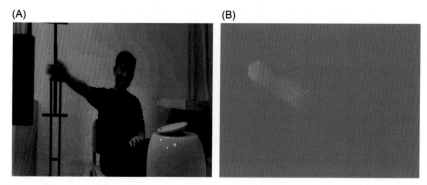

Figure 6.9 Optical flow data corresponding to visible light data. (A) Visible light data showing a person gesturing with their right arm. (B) Corresponding optical flow data highlighting arm movement.

(TSNs) based on the two-stream network, which is used for video action recognition. The structure of TSN is a two-stream structure. One stream is a spatial convolutional network used to learn image dimension information, and the other stream is a temporal convolutional network used to learn temporal dimension information. This method divides a video into multiple segments and randomly samples an RGB image for each segment as the input of the spatial convolution network. The input of the temporal convolutional network is the optical flow data corresponding to the segment. The network will give its preliminary prediction of the behavioral category for each segment and finally fuse the prediction results of all segments to obtain the predicted category of the entire video.

Narayana et al. [21] proposed a FOANet based on multichannel fusion. The network uses four modal data as input, including RGB data, depth data, optical flow data generated by RGB data (RGB flow), and optical flow data generated by depth data (depth flow). Each modality uses a network to extract global features and a spatial attention mechanism to extract left-hand and right-hand features. Finally, a sparse network is used to fuse these features to obtain the final classification result.

6.1.5 Saliency data

Generally speaking, saliency algorithms are mostly based on human attention when observing things to extract more obvious areas in the image. Depending on whether bionics theory is used, saliency algorithms can be divided into biology-based methods and statistics-based methods. Some algorithms combine the two to extract saliency targets from images.

Among biology-based methods, the biological feasibility architecture proposed by Koch et al. [22] is relatively representative. Based on this architecture, Itti et al. [23] use the difference of Gaussians (DoG) to determine the contrast between the central area and surrounding areas. Frintrop et al. [24] proposed using a square filter to determine the contrast between the central area and the surrounding area based on the work of Itti et al., and used an integral map to improve the operation speed. Statistics-based methods generally do not rely on bionic theory. For example, Ma et al. [25] and Achanta et al. [26] utilize the feature distance between the central area and surrounding areas to estimate saliency. Hu et al. [27] use histogram threshold features and heuristic methods to extract salient targets. Some methods combine the two to achieve the extraction of saliency targets. For example, Harel et al. [28] employ methods based on biological information for feature mapping but utilize statistics-based graph methods for normalization.

This section will mainly introduce the saliency estimation method proposed by Achanta et al. [29]. The method uses color and brightness features to calculate the contrast of the center and the surrounding areas based on the concept of frequency tuning. When performing saliency estimation, the saliency filter needs to meet the following requirements:

1. Emphasize the largest salient object.
2. Highlight the entire prominent area evenly.
3. Establish clear boundaries for salient objects.
4. Remove high-frequency noise caused by interference such as texture and noise, and block artifacts.
5. Efficiently output clear saliency images.

To highlight the target object, lower-frequency features in the original image need to be considered. To clarify the boundary between the target and the background, it is necessary to preserve the high-frequency areas in the original image. To resolve high-frequency noise caused by interference, such as texture, noise, and blocking, the highest frequency regions need to be ignored. Therefore, this method uses multiple DoG filters and combines their outputs over a continuous bandwidth. The DoG filter equation is shown in Formula (6.7):

$$DoG(x, y) = \frac{1}{2\pi} \left[\frac{1}{\sigma_1^2} e^{-\frac{(x^2+y^2)}{2\sigma_1^2}} - \frac{1}{\sigma_2^2} e^{-\frac{(x^2+y^2)}{2\sigma_2^2}} \right]$$

$$= G(x, y, \sigma_1) - G(x, y, \sigma_2)$$

(6.7)

where σ_1 and σ_2 are the standard deviation of the gaussian distribution, and $\sigma_1 < \sigma_2$. Since the DoG filter is simple, its bandwidth is controlled by the ratio of $\sigma_1 : \sigma_2$. If $\sigma_1 = \rho\sigma$, $\sigma_2 = \sigma$ are defined, the sum of multiple DoG filters with standard deviation ratios ρ is as shown in Formula (6.8):

$$\sum_{n=0}^{N-1} G(x, y, \rho^{n+1}\sigma) - G(x, y, \rho^{n}\sigma) = G(x, y, \sigma\rho^{N}) - G(x, y, \sigma) \qquad (6.8)$$

let $K = \rho^{N}$, a DoG filter with a wider frequency band can be obtained by using a larger value of K. To make the K larger, it is necessary to increase σ_1 to infinity. At this point, filtering the image can be regarded as computing the average value of the entire image. To remove high-frequency noise and texture, σ_2 needs to use a small Gaussian kernel. Therefore, the calculation method of the saliency map is as shown in Formula (6.9).

$$S(x, y) = ||I_{\mu} - I_{\omega_{hc}}(x, y)|| \qquad (6.9)$$

where I_{μ} is the arithmetic mean pixel value of the original image, $I_{\omega_{hc}}(x, y)$ is a Gaussian blurred version of the original image, and $|| \cdot ||$ is the L2 norm. The saliency image obtained by the above method is shown in Fig. 6.10.

Since the saliency algorithm processes images, it must first decompose each video into an image sequence, then obtain a saliency map for each frame of the image, and finally combine the obtained saliency images of each frame in order. The video processed using the saliency algorithm can be obtained.

Based on saliency data, Duan et al. [30] propose a two-stream network architecture for multimodal data fusion, integrating RGB data, depth data,

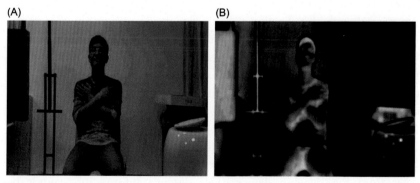

Figure 6.10 Visible light data and corresponding saliency data. (A) Original data in visible light. (B) Corresponding saliency map highlighting areas of visual interest or importance in the scene.

and saliency data. This architecture is used to solve the loss of 3D structural information and reduce interference from background, noise, and other external factors. The network is divided into two parts: two-stream consensus-voting network (2SCVN) and 3D depth-saliency stream network (3DDSN). Through two streams, 2SCVN learns temporal and spatial information from the given input. The spatial stream in 2SCVN uses RGB images and depth images as input, while the temporal stream uses RGB images and optical flow images as input. The prediction scores of the spatial stream and the temporal stream are jointly used as the prediction results of 2SCVN. To implicitly learn temporal and spatial information, 3DDSN uses depth images and saliency images. Finally, the scores of 2SCVN and 3DDSN are further integrated as the final prediction result.

Miao et al. [31] propose a multimodal gesture recognition method based on the ResC3D network [32] on large-scale datasets. The method applies video enhancement to RGB data and depth data to eliminate noise and lighting effects. Based on this, it utilizes motion intensity as a criterion and incorporates a keyframe attention mechanism to extract the most representative frames for gesture recognition. Subsequently, multimodal data, including RGB data, depth data, and optical flow data generated from RGB data, is fed into the ResC3D network to extract spatiotemporal features. Finally, feature fusion is achieved through canonical correlation analysis, and the ultimate recognition result is obtained using a linear SVM classifier.

6.2 Fusion algorithm of different modality data

In general, each different source or form of data is a modality. Each of the data types described in Section 6.1 is a data mode commonly used in the field of gesture recognition. Multimodal fusion is a strategy that combines two or more modality data in a certain way. Despite certain salient features, such as the outline of objects, showing consistency across different modality data, there are often large differences in details between different modality data.

In the field of gesture recognition, visible light images (RGB images) can better represent the texture features of the target. Compared with RGB images, depth images are more able to reflect the distance of the target from the imaging device. This distance information cannot be provided by the traditional RGB modality. More importantly, the depth data can eliminate the interference of light, shadows, and environmental changes. The optical flow modality can effectively obtain the motion information of gestures, which is very important in dynamic gesture recognition tasks based on video data. Therefore, if the multimodal information can be reasonably combined, more discriminative and robust multimodal features can be obtained, providing a more comprehensive description of gesture movements.

The key to deep learning with multimodal data lies in the application of multimodal fusion methods. Based on the degree of abstraction of fused data, multimodal fusion methods can be categorized into data-level fusion, feature-level fusion, decision-level fusion, and hybrid fusion [33]. Data-level fusion refers to the direct fusion of raw data from multiple input modes. Feature-level fusion refers to the fusion of features extracted through neural networks or algorithms and then using the fused features as input for classification or regression tasks (usually only connecting the representations of various modality features). Decision-level fusion means that the final result, such as the probability of output classification, is obtained directly with the data of each mode, and then the results of different modes are compared or combined according to certain rules to obtain a comprehensive result. Hybrid fusion involves combining two or more fusion methods simultaneously at different stages of the model. This section takes gesture recognition as the starting point to introduce the above fusion methods.

6.2.1 Data-level fusion

As shown in Fig. 6.11, data-level fusion is the most foundational fusion strategy. This fusion strategy directly fuses raw data, followed by feature analysis and evaluation of the fused data.

The main advantage of data-level fusion is that the details of the raw data are preserved to the maximum extent. The disadvantage of this method lies in the large amount of raw data that needs to be processed and the high time complexity of fusion. On the other hand, it is required to have pixel-level registration accuracy between different modalities of information; otherwise, it will affect the subsequent processing due to the noise caused by the difference in object contours in the data of different modalities. From Fig. 6.12, it can be seen that, due to the lack of registration between RGB data and depth data, there is a significant phenomenon of ghosting during fusion. Therefore, data-level fusion may produce useless results.

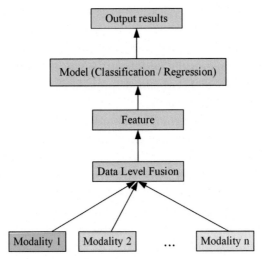

Figure 6.11 Data-level fusion method.

Figure 6.12 Result of single-frame data-level fusion of unregistered RGB and depth videos.

6.2.2 Feature-level fusion

As shown in Fig. 6.13, feature-level fusion combines different modalities of raw data after the raw data have undergone feature extraction through a neural network or manual methods. As a result there is no need to unify the data form, and the problem of scale inconsistency between the raw

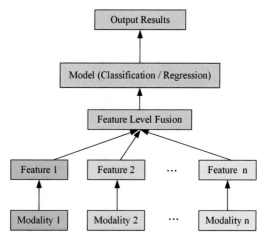

Figure 6.13 Feature-level fusion method.

data of each modality can be avoided. At the same time, feature-level fusion achieves information compression to a certain extent, which is conducive to reducing the time complexity of the algorithm. The following will introduce several feature-level fusion methods and their applications in gesture recognition.

6.2.2.1 Feature-level fusion method
6.2.2.1.1 Pointwise addition strategy and feature-concatenation strategy

The most classic feature-level fusion methods include pointwise addition and concatenation of features. From Fig. 6.14, it can be observed that pointwise addition aligns feature vectors of different modalities and adds elements at the same position. Feature concatenation is the concatenation of two different modality features into a longer feature vector. Therefore, compared with feature concatenation, pointwise addition requires that the dimensions of the fused vectors themselves be consistent.

Next, we use formulas to specify the different fusion methods. Assuming two sets of feature vectors are $X = [X_1, X_2, \ldots, X_n]$ and $Y = [Y_1, Y_2, \ldots, Y_n]$, then the fusion feature Z_{add} of the pointwise addition strategy can be expressed as:

$$Z_{\text{add}} = \sum_{i=1}^{n}(X_i + Y_i) * K = \sum_{i=1}^{n} X_i * K + \sum_{i=1}^{n} Y_i * K \qquad (6.10)$$

where $*$ represents convolution; K represents convolution kernel.

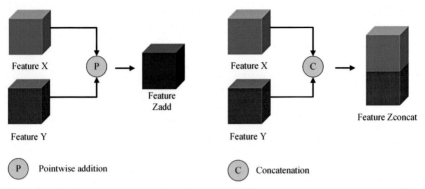

Figure 6.14 Fusion method of pointwise addition strategy and concatenation strategy.

The fusion feature Z_{concat} of feature series can be expressed as:

$$Z_{\text{concat}} = \sum_{i=1}^{n} X_i * K_X \oplus \sum_{i=1}^{n} Y_i * K_Y \tag{6.11}$$

where K_X represents the convolution kernel corresponding to the feature vector X, and K_Y represents the convolution kernel corresponding to the feature vector Y.

In general, the pointwise addition method does not change the dimension of the feature, so it does not increase the computational complexity during subsequent processing. However, since this method directly adds the values of each element, it is essentially a compromise strategy, which may lose information that is closely related to the final result. However, the feature-series method can retain all the features of different modality data and provide sufficient information for the final classification. However, this method increases the length of features, which is not conducive to the efficient operation of the algorithm.

6.2.2.1.2 Fusion method based on statistical analysis features

Although the above two fusion methods are easy to implement, they simply overlay features without considering the correlation of features at the same position. The approach does not fully leverage the complementarity of different model data and thus may not necessarily achieve optimal results. A feasible strategy is to use statistical analysis methods to study the association between different modality features and then use this association to fuse.

Canonical correlation analysis (CCA) is a statistical method in multivariate analysis that studies the correlation between two sets of random variables [34]. CCA works by projecting two sets of feature vectors to find the projection direction that maximizes their correlation. Then the weight of the feature is obtained in the corresponding projection direction, and the weighted fusion of the feature vector is performed. This method finds the projection direction that maximizes the correlation between the two sets of feature vectors before fusion, thus effectively eliminating redundant information and further improving the effectiveness and conciseness of the fused features.

Suppose $\mathbf{X} = [x_1, x_2, \ldots, x_m]$, $x_i \in R^m$ and $\mathbf{Y} = [y_1, y_2, \ldots, y_n], y_j \in R^n$ represent two features in different modes in the gesture recognition problem. Then their covariance matrix $\mathbf{C}$ is expressed as:

$$\mathbf{C} = \begin{pmatrix} \mathrm{Var}(\mathbf{X}) & \mathrm{Cov}(\mathbf{X}, \mathbf{Y}) \\ \mathrm{Cov}(\mathbf{Y}, \mathbf{X}) & \mathrm{Var}(\mathbf{Y}) \end{pmatrix} = \begin{pmatrix} \mathbf{C}_{xx} & \mathbf{C}_{xy} \\ \mathbf{C}_{yx} & \mathbf{C}_{yy} \end{pmatrix} \tag{6.12}$$

where $\mathbf{C}_{xx} = \mathrm{Var}(\mathbf{X})$ and $\mathbf{C}_{yy} = \mathrm{Var}(\mathbf{Y})$ represent the intra–class covariance matrices of $\mathbf{X}$ and $\mathbf{Y}$, $\mathbf{C}_{xy} = \mathrm{Cov}(\mathbf{X}, \mathbf{Y})$ represents the interclass covariance matrices of $\mathbf{X}$ and $\mathbf{Y}$, and $\mathbf{C}_{yx} = \mathbf{C}_{xy}^T$.

The CCA algorithm first finds a pair of projection directions α_1 and β_1 to make the linear combination $\mathbf{u}_1 = \alpha_1^T \mathbf{X}$ and $\mathbf{v}_1 = \beta_1^T \mathbf{Y}$ to have the maximum correlation; $\mathbf{u}_1$ and $\mathbf{v}_1$ are the first pair of typical variables. Similarly, the second pair of projection directions α_2 and β_2 are found to obtain the second pair of typical variables $\mathbf{u}_2$ and $\mathbf{v}_2$, so that they are not correlated with the first pair of typical variables $\mathbf{u}_1$ and $\mathbf{v}_1$, and there is the greatest correlation between $\mathbf{u}_2$ and $\mathbf{v}_2$. This goes on until the min (m, n) step (i.e., the minimum number of elements in both sets of vectors) is reached, which is the projection direction that makes $\mathbf{X}$ and $\mathbf{Y}$ most correlated.

The correlation coefficient between the projection directions α and β is obtained by maximizing the simple correlation coefficient between the two, that is, $\mathrm{Cov}(\alpha, \beta)$. The criterion for determining the correlation coefficient is shown in Formula (6.13):

$$\mathrm{Cov}(\alpha, \beta) = \frac{\alpha^T \mathbf{C}_{xy} \beta}{\sqrt{\alpha^T \mathbf{C}_{xx}{}^T \alpha \beta^T \mathbf{C}_{yy} \beta}} \tag{6.13}$$

CCA can be expressed as a solution to the following optimization problem:

$$\text{Cov}(\alpha,\beta) = \text{argmax}_{\alpha,\beta}\,(\alpha^{\mathrm{T}}\mathbf{C}_{xy}\beta)$$

$$s.t.\ \ \alpha^{\mathrm{T}}\mathbf{C}_{xx}\alpha = \beta^{\mathrm{T}}\mathbf{C}_{yy}\beta = 1 \tag{6.14}$$

This problem can be solved using the Lagrange multiplier method, let:

$$L(\alpha,\beta) = \alpha^{\mathrm{T}}\mathbf{C}_{xy}\beta - \frac{\lambda_1}{2}\left(\alpha^{\mathrm{T}}\mathbf{C}_{xx}^{\mathrm{T}}\alpha - 1\right) - \frac{\lambda_2}{2}\left(\beta^{\mathrm{T}}\mathbf{C}_{yy}\beta - 1\right) \tag{6.15}$$

where λ_1 and λ_2 are Lagrange multipliers. Finding $\text{Cov}(\alpha,\beta)$ becomes the eigenvalue problem of solving Formula (6.16):

$$\begin{aligned}\mathbf{C}_{yx}\mathbf{C}_{xx}^{-1}\mathbf{C}_{xy}\alpha &= \lambda^2\mathbf{C}_{yy}\beta \\ \mathbf{C}_{yx}\mathbf{C}_{xx}^{-1}\mathbf{C}_{xy}\alpha &= \lambda^2\mathbf{C}_{yy}\beta\end{aligned} \tag{6.16}$$

If n is the number of nonnegative eigenvalues of $\mathbf{C}_{xy}\mathbf{C}_{yy}^{-1}\mathbf{C}_{xx}$, at most n pairs of solutions can be obtained. Assuming that the eigenvalues obtained are nonincreasing:

The order is $\lambda_1 \ge \lambda_2 \ge \ldots \ge \lambda_n \ge 0$, and the eigenvectors corresponding to nonzero eigenvalues $d \le \text{rank}\,(\mathbf{S}_{xy})$ are taken as the typical projection direction.

The goal of the typical correlation analysis algorithm is finally transformed into a convex optimization process, and only the maximum value of the optimization goal is required, and then the typical correlation discrimination feature Z of multidimensional X and Y is obtained. By integrating the features of different modes, the correlation information between the two can be preserved as much as possible.

6.2.2.2 Application of feature-level fusion in gesture recognition

Feature-level fusion is widely applied in gesture recognition algorithms. Li et al. [35] proposed a gesture recognition algorithm based on RGB-D multimodal data. Regarding the issue of how to efficiently utilize multimodal data, Li et al. attempted a data-level fusion method, but video data of different modalities were not registered, and the data-level fusion method could not obtain effective fusion data. Subsequently, Li et al. used the feature-level fusion method to fuse the RGB data features and depth data features. As shown in Table 6.1, Li et al. used two fusion strategies, pointwise addition and concatenation, to fuse multimodal data. It can be seen from the test results that, compared with using any single modality data, the method of blending multimodal data can significantly improve recognition accuracy. It can also be seen that the results of the two fusion strategies are basically the same, but the

Table 6.1 Comparison of fusion strategies in Li algorithm [34].

Type of data	RGB data	Depth data	Pointwise	Concatenation
Accuracy	37.3%	40.5%	49.0%	49.2%

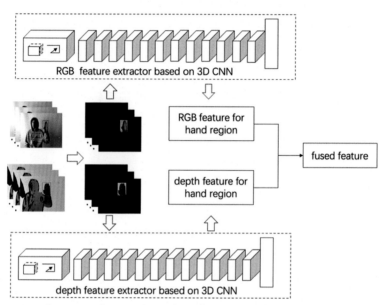

Figure 6.15 Structure of Liu et al.'s multimodal gesture recognition network [36].

concatenation strategy is slightly better than the pointwise addition strategy. Because the feature-concatenation strategy can obtain all feature information from various modalities, while the pointwise addition strategy tends to balance the modal information, it may risk losing information that is more relevant to the final result Fig. 6.15.

When Liu et al. [36] tackled the problem of continuous gesture recognition [37], they also utilized a feature-level fusion method to fuse RGB and depth modality data. As shown in Fig. 6.16, Liu et al. initially segmented continuous gestures to obtain independent gesture video clips and transformed the task into the independent gesture recognition problem, which is the same as Li et al. For each video clip, only the hand and facial regions are retained through facial and hand detection. Subsequently, in order to deeply explore complementary multimodal data information, Liu et al. fused two modalities of data through feature concatenation to enhance the final recognition performance.

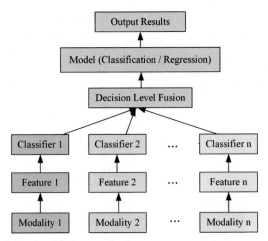

Figure 6.16 Decision-level fusion method.

Table 6.2 Comparison of fusion strategies in Liu algorithm [36].

Feature Type of data	RGB	Depth	Concatenation
Global feature	36.94%	35.34%	44.22%
Hand feature	43.8%	44.73%	50.11%
Hand feature + face feature	45.94%	46.6%	51.53%

Liu et al. used a feature–concatenation strategy to concatenate and fuse the feature vectors of RGB data and depth data. The process can be expressed as:

$$F = fc_{\text{rgb}} \oplus fc_{\text{depth}} \tag{6.17}$$

where fc_{rgb} and fc_{depth} represent the features obtained by the model based on the corresponding RGB data and depth data; $\oplus$ is called the series operator; and F is the final fused feature.

As shown in Table 6.2, Liu et al. separately tested the performance of different features through the feature concatenation method for fusion. It can be clearly seen from the results in Table 6.2 that whether only hand features are considered, or both hand and face features are considered, or global features are extracted only from the original video, compared with any single modality (RGB data or depth data), the accuracy rate can be increased by more than 5% using the feature series fusion strategy.

In addition, Miao et al. [31] proposed a multimodal gesture recognition method based on the ResC3D network. In this method, Miao et al.

Table 6.3 Miao comparison of fusion strategies in Miao algorithm [31].

Modal/ fusion methods	RGB data	Depth data	Optical flow data	Pointwise	Concatenation	CCA fusion
Accuracy	45.07%	48.44%	44.45%	57.88%	58.35%	64.11%

introduced the CCA strategy to obtain the fusion parameters of different modality features. The comparison of the effects of different fusion methods is shown in Table 6.3.

As shown in Table 6.3, Miao et al. studied fusion strategies such as mean features, feature concatenation, and CCA. Experimental results show that, compared with the results of any single modality, multimodal fusion has a significant improvement in accuracy. Meanwhile, it can also be seen that the fusion strategy based on CCA is significantly better than the other two fusion strategies. The reason is that the fusion strategy based on CCA maximizes the correlation between different modality features, thereby eliminating redundant information to the greatest extent and getting the best fusion effect.

6.2.3 Decision-level fusion

Decision-level fusion involves the logical or statistical reasoning process applied to multiple sets of data. Decision-level fusion algorithm is essentially a fusion at the classifier level, providing a basis for controlling decisions. As shown in Fig. 6.16, these algorithms initially input sample data into different classifiers for preliminary decisions. Subsequently, the decision results from each classifier undergo decision-level fusion processing to obtain the final joint decision result.

6.2.3.1 Strategies of decision-level fusion

The most classic decision-level fusion algorithm is the score fusion strategy. Score fusion strategies include average-score fusion strategy, weight-score fusion strategy, max-score fusion strategy, etc. The average-score fusion strategy averages the results of multiple classifiers to obtain a smooth result. The weight-score fusion is a further extension of the average-score fusion strategy. Due to variations in the feature learning capabilities of different classifiers, which in turn affect the final classification results, different weights are used to represent the importance of each classifier to obtain more reasonable results. The max-score fusion strategy is to select the classification result with the highest probability among multiple classifiers. The fusion strategies have the advantages of simplicity, ease of implementation, and fast computing speed.

6.2.3.2 Application of decision-level fusion method in gesture recognition

When tackling gesture recognition problems, Zhang et al. [38] used the score-fusion strategy in the decision-level fusion algorithm to fuse the spatio-temporal information between frames in the video, effectively improving the performance of gesture recognition. As shown in Fig. 6.17, Zhang et al. divided the continuous gesture video into several independent gesture segments, used a 3D convolutional neural network to extract spatiotemporal features, used convLSTM to learn the spatiotemporal features of these segments, used 2D CNN to further characterize extraction, obtained the classification results of each video clip through the fully connected layer, and finally used the fractional fusion strategy to fuse the classification results of each video clip to obtain the gesture classification results.

As shown in Table 6.4, Zhang et al. separately employ the average score-fusion strategy and the max score-fusion strategy between single

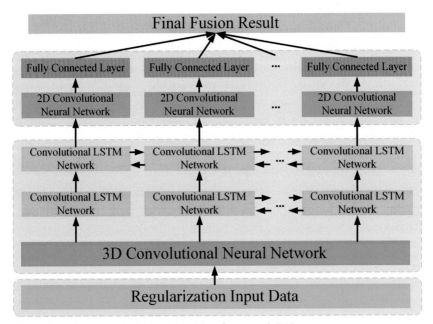

Figure 6.17 Gesture recognition algorithm framework [38].

Table 6.4 Comparison of fusion strategies in Zhang's algorithm [38].

Fusion strategy Type of data	RGB	Depth	Fusion results
Max–score fusion	50.48%	47.93%	54.55%
Average-score fusion	50.97%	48.89%	55.29%

modality and multimodality. It can be observed from the experimental results that average fusion shows better results in any modality, and compared with the results of any single modality, the fusion of multimodal data further enhances the accuracy of recognition.

Wang et al. [39] also adopted the score-fusion strategy when dealing with continuous gesture recognition problems. Different from the spatiotemporal-information fusion based on the same network proposed by Liu et al. in [36], Wang et al. used different networks to perform decision-level fusion of information at different spatial levels (body and hand). As shown in Fig. 6.18, Wang et al. constructed dynamic images of the body and hands based on RGB-D continuous frames, inputting them into a convolutional neural network. Simultaneously, the same data is input into a 3D convolutional long short-term memory network. Eventually, the results of the two classifiers are fused using an average score-fusion strategy to enhance the final recognition performance.

As shown in Fig. 6.18, Wang et al. performed a decision-level fusion, which is an average score-fusion strategy to combine two classifiers. It can be observed from the experimental results that, compared with a single classifier, the fusion of two classifiers increases the accuracy by 4% to 7%. This fusion method can fully make use of features learned by different classifiers, thereby improving recognition accuracy.

6.2.4 Other fusion methods

As shown in Fig. 6.19, in addition to the above-mentioned fusion algorithms, there are also some special fusion algorithms, for example, neural network-based fusion algorithms. The fusion algorithm based on the neural network converts different modality data into high-dimensional features and then transmits the obtained high-dimensional features to the neural network for fusion. Due to the diversity and adaptability of the neural network model structures, the network fusion method is more flexible and has been widely applied in fields such as multimedia [40], face recognition [41], and gesture recognition [21].

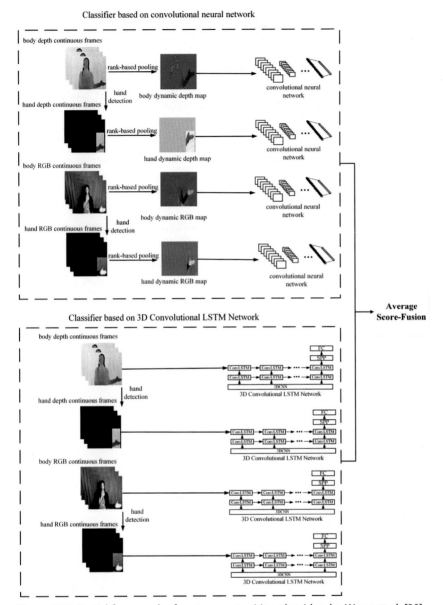

Figure 6.18 Partial framework of gesture recognition algorithm by Wang et al. [39].

6.2.4.1 Method of application

Narayana et al. [21] designed an FOANet framework for gesture recognition problems and proposed a new fusion method called sparse-network

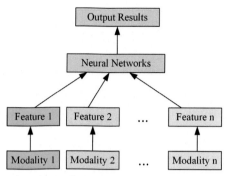

Figure 6.19 Fusion method based on neural network.

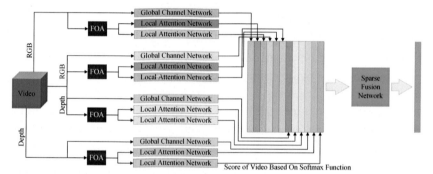

Figure 6.20 FOANet architecture [20].

fusion. In this network framework, feature extraction is performed on depth, depth data stream, visible light data, and visible light data stream, and the extracted features are fused with a sparse network. The network framework is shown in Fig. 6.20.

In Fig. 6.20, Narayana et al. concatenated the 12 feature vectors generated by the 12 network channels to form preliminary features. Narayana et al. further analyzed the movement characteristics of gestures. For example, diving as an action in the water can be seen from a distance, so it requires large arm movements, while saluting is a small movement with one hand. Therefore, the diving gesture needs to emphasize global features, while the right-hand features dominate in the salute gesture and local features are emphasized. FOANet uses sparsely connected neural layers. The sparse-network layer performs weight learning based on the relative importance of spatial regions and data modalities and then selects the best gesture categories.

Table 6.5 Comparison of fusion strategies.

Fusion method	Results on validation set		Results on test set	
	12 channels	7 channels	12 channels	7 channels
Sparse fusion	80.96%	77.31%	82.07%	78.90%
Average (pointwise addition)	67.38%	69.06%	70.37%	71.93
Concatenation	56.03%	55.29%	59.44%	58.84%

To evaluate the sparse network fusion strategy, as shown in Table 6.5, Narayana et al. conducted comparative experiments on the CGD IsoGD dataset and compared the sparse network fusion strategy with the average fusion strategy. The experimental results show that the sparse–network fusion strategy improves gesture recognition accuracy by 11.7%, proving the effectiveness of the sparse-network fusion strategy.

The fusion methods mentioned above each have their own advantages and disadvantages. Data-level fusion requires processing a large amount of data in advance, which takes a long time, is expensive, and has poor real-time performance. Feature-level fusion focuses on capturing the relationship between features but is prone to overfitting. The decision-level fusion algorithm can better handle the overfitting problem, but there is more information loss in the algorithm. Researchers need to choose the fusion method based on specific application problems and research content.

6.3 Summary

The chapter introduces the data and corresponding generation methods of six different modes of RGB, depth, infrared, skeleton, optical flow, and saliency data that are more common in gesture recognition. It explains the fusion methods from the data level, feature level, and decision level. Furthermore several specific examples show how to improve recognition performance through multimodal fusion algorithms in gesture recognition.

References

[1] Three Hackers, Depth image acquisition principle [EB/OL].(三名狂客. 深度图像的获取原理 [EB/OL].) (in Chinese).
[2] E. Ricci, W. Ouyang, X. Wang, et al., Monocular depth estimation using multi-scale continuous CRFs as sequential deep networks, IEEE Transactions on Pattern Analysis and Machine 41 (6) (2018) 1426−1440.

[3] F. Dominio, M. Donadeo, G. Marin, et al., Hand gesture recognition with depth data, in: Proceedings of ACM/IEEE International Workshop on Analysis and Retrieval of Tracked Events and Motion in Imagery Stream, 2013, pp. 9–16.

[4] D.Q. Leite, J.C. Duarte, L.P. Neves, et al., Hand gesture recognition from depth and infrared Kinect data for CAVE applications interaction, Multimedia Tools and Applications 76 (20) (2017) 20423–20455.

[5] D.G. Lowe, Distinctive image features from scale-invariant keypoints, International Journal of Computer Vision 60 (2) (2004) 91–110.

[6] T. Mantecón, C.R. Del-Blanco, F. Jaureguizar, et al., A real-time gesture recognition system using near-infrared imagery, PLoS One 14 (10) (2019) e0223320.

[7] G. Rogez, C. Schmid, Mocap-guided data augmentation for 3D pose estimation in the wild, in: Proceedings on Advances in Neural Information Processing Systems, 2016, pp. 3108–3116.

[8] J. Shotton, A. Fitzgibbon, M. Cook, et al., Real-time human pose recognition in parts from single depth images, Proceedings of IEEE Conference on Computer Vision and Pattern Recognition. IEEE (2011) 1297–1304.

[9] Z. Cao, T. Simon, S.E. Wei, et al., Realtime multi-person 2D pose estimation using part affinity fields, arXiv preprint arXiv:1611.08050, 2016.

[10] D. Pavllo, C. Feichtenhofer, D. Grangier, et al., 3D human pose estimation in video with temporal convolutions and semi-supervised training. arXiv preprint arXiv:1811.11742, 2018.

[11] SIGAI_csdn, Summary of Human Skeleton Keypoint Detection [EB/OL]. https://blog.csdn.net/sigai_csdn/article/details/80650411, 2018 (SIGAI_csdn. 人体骨骼关键点检测综述[EB/OL].) (in Chinese).

[12] W. Li, Traffic directing gesture recognition based on skeletonization and template matching, Zhejiang University of Technology, Zhejiang, 2011 (李文杰. 基于骨架化和模板匹配的交通指挥手势识别. 浙江: 浙江工业大学, 2011) (in Chinese).

[13] Z. Cao, G. Hidalgo, T. Simon, et al., OpenPose: realtime multi-person 2D pose estimation using Part Affinity Fields, IEEE Transactions on Pattern Analysis and Machine Intelligence 43 (1) (2019) 172–186.

[14] Q. De Smedt, H. Wannous, J.P. Vandeborre, Skeleton-based dynamic hand gesture recognition, in: Proceedings of IEEE Conference on Computer Vision and Pattern Recognition Workshops, 2016, pp. 1–9.

[15] J. Hou, G. Wang, X. Chen, et al., Proceedings of European Conference on Computer Vision Workshops, 2018, pp. 1–15.

[16] B. Ionescu, D. Coquin, P. Lambert, et al., Dynamic hand gesture recognition using the skeleton of the hand, EURASIP Journal on Advances in Signal Processing 2005 (13) (2005) 1–9.

[17] W. Chong, C.S. Chow. A new hand gesture recognition algorithm based on joint color-depth Superpixel Earth Mover's Distance, in: Proceedings of International Workshop on Cognitive Information Processing, IEEE, 2014, pp. 1–6.

[18] B.K.P. Horn, B.G. Schunck, Determining optical flow, Artificial Intelligence 17 (1–3) (1981) 185–203.

[19] T. Brox, A. Bruhn, N. Papenberg, et al., High accuracy optical flow estimation based on a theory for warping, in: Proceedings of European Conference on Computer Vision, Springer, 2004, pp. 25–36.

[20] L. Wang, Y. Xiong, Z. Wang, et al., Temporal segment networks: towards good practices for deep action recognition, in: Proceedings of European Conference on Computer Vision, Springer, 2016, pp. 20–36.

[21] P. Narayana, R. Beveridge, B.A. Draper, Gesture recognition: focus on the hands, in: Proceedings of IEEE Conference on Computer Vision and Pattern Recognition, 2018, pp. 5235−5244.

[22] C. Koch, S. Ullman, Shifts in selective visual attention: towards the underlying neural circuitry, in: Matters of intelligence, Springer, Dordrecht, 1987, pp. 115−141.

[23] L. Itti, C. Koch, E. Niebur, A model of saliency-based visual attention for rapid scene analysis, IEEE Transactions on Pattern Analysis and Machine Intelligence 20 (11) (1998) 1254−1259.

[24] S. Frintrop, M. Klodt, E. Rome, A real-time visual attention system using integral images, in: Proceedings of International Conference on Computer Vision Systems, 2007, pp. 1−10.

[25] Y.-F. Ma, H.-J. Zhang, Contrast-based image attention analysis by using fuzzy growing, in: Proceedings of ACM International Conference on Multimedia, 2003, pp. 374−381.

[26] R. Achanta, F. Estrada, P. Wils et al., Salient region detection and segmentation, in: Proceedings of International Conference on Computer Vision Systems, Springer, 2008, pp. 66−75.

[27] H. Yiqun, X. Xing, M. Wei-Ying, et al., Salient region detection using weighted feature maps based on the human visual attention model, in: Proceedings of Pacific-Rim Conference on Multimedia, Springer, Berlin, Heidelberg, 2004, pp. 993−1000.

[28] J. Harel, C. Koch, P. Perona, Graph-based visual saliency, in: Proceedings of Advance in Neural Information Processing Systems, 2007, pp. 1−8.

[29] R. Achanta, S. Hemami, F. Estrada, et al., Frequency-tuned salient region detection, Proceedings of IEEE Conference on Computer Vision and Pattern Recognition, IEEE, 2009, pp. 1597−1604.

[30] J. Duan, J. Wan, S. Zhou, et al., A unified framework for multi-modal isolated gesture recognition, ACM Transactions on Multimedia Computing, Communications, and Applications 14 (1) (2018) 1−16.

[31] Q. Miao, Y. Li, W. Ouyang, et al., Multimodal gesture recognition based on the RESC3D network, in: Proceedings of IEEE International Conference on Computer Vision Workshops. 2017, pp. 3047−3055.

[32] D. Tran, J. Ray, Z. Shou, et al., Convnet architecture search for spatiotemporal feature learning. arXiv preprint arXiv:1708.05038, 2017.

[33] J. He, C. Zhang, X. Li, A review of research on multi-modal fusion technology for deep learning, Computer Engineering 46 (5) (2020) 1−11.

[34] 李洪亮,马启明,杜栓平.一种基于典型相关分析的特征融合算法.声学与电子工程 2015 (1) 20−23.

[35] Y. Li, Q. Miao, T. Kuan, et al., Large-scale gesture recognition with a fusion of RGB-D data based on the C3D model, in: Proceedings of International Conference on Pattern Recognition, IEEE, 2016, pp. 25−30.

[36] Z. Liu, X. Chai, L. Zhuang, et al., Continuous gesture recognition with hand-oriented spatiotemporal feature, in: Proceedings of IEEE International Conference on Computer Vision Workshops, 2017, pp. 3056−3064.

[37] J. Wan, Y. Zhao, Z. Shuai, et al., Chalearn looking at people rgb-d isolated and continuous datasets for gesture recognition, in: Proceedings of IEEE Conference on Computer Vision and Pattern Recognition Workshops, 2016, pp. 56−64.

[38] L. Zhang, G. Zhu, P. Shen, et al., Learning spatiotemporal features using 3dcnn and convolutional lstm for gesture recognition, in: Proceedings of IEEE International Conference on Computer Vision Workshops, 2017, pp. 3120−3128.

[39] H. Wang, P. Wang, Z. Song, et al., Large-scale multimodal gesture recognition using heterogeneous networks, in: Proceedings of IEEE International Conference on Computer Vision Workshops, 2017, pp. 3129−3137.

[40] Z.-Z. Lan, L. Bao, S.I. Yu, et al., Multimedia classification and event detection using double fusion, Multimedia Tools and Applications 71 (1) (2014) 333−347.

[41] J. Liu, C. Fang, C. Wu, A fusion face recognition approach based on 7-layer deep learning neural network, Journal of Electrical and Computer Engineering (2016).

CHAPTER 7

Gesture recognition and attention mechanisms

7.1 Concept of attention mechanism

7.1.1 Progress in the study of attention mechanism

The emergence of attention mechanisms is inextricably linked to the study of human vision. Their application in deep learning started in 2014 with Google DeepMind's *Recurrent Models of Visual Attention* [1]. This article has used attention mechanisms in the work on image classification using RNN models and has achieved good results. In 2017, Google published the paper *Attention is All You Need* [2], which used attention mechanisms to learn text representation in machine translation problems. After this, attention mechanisms have been widely used in the field of natural language processing. Influenced by this, gesture recognition tasks have also started to borrow attention algorithms from natural language processing. For example, Wenjie Li [3] and Wang et al. [4] have used attention mechanisms to highlight gesture-related regions such as hands and elbows in images or videos, and the processed data showed significant improvement in recognition results.

7.1.2 Human visual attention

The attention mechanism in deep learning is closely related to human visual attention. First, human attention is limited due to physiological limitations, so it is impossible for humans to pay attention to all the details in a scene. In addition, since a large amount of information is irrelevant to what people care about when observing things, paying selective attention to some scenes can help people understand things better. For example, when talking, people may pay more attention to the expressions and body language of the person they are talking to, while ignoring other people and background information; when viewing a landscape, people pay more attention to the landscape than the passing tourists. In other words, humans focus on areas relevant to the current activity, also known as the attention mechanism. This is a long-term survival strategy—a way

Gesture Recognition
DOI: https://doi.org/10.1016/B978-0-443-28959-0.00001-7
155

Figure 7.1 Schematic representation of human attention during image observation.

to quickly select high-quality data from a large amount of data using limited access resources. As shown in Fig. 7.1, the higher the luminance, the higher the probability that people will stay at that location when observing the image. People pay more attention to areas with clearer textures and more obvious targets, such as grass, trees, and swans in the near field, rather than less clear and unclear areas, such as houses covered by haze in the far field.

7.1.3 Using attention mechanisms in computer vision

In computer vision, the attention mechanism selects the most relevant information for the task by mimicking the process of human observation of things. Generally speaking, when humans observe things, they not only obtain global information from the whole but also detailed information from the localities that are relevant to the current task.

Taking gesture recognition as an example, we need to focus more on the climax part after the action starts and the whole area of the hands, arms, and upper part of the body in the picture, while the background and facial expressions in the picture have little influence on our final result. The feature information that ultimately determines the gesture classification is composed of the effective information per unit time as well as the temporal information of the context, that is, a combination of a series of effective information in sequential order. Just like when a person pays attention to a series of actions or listens to a conversation, they do not need to pay full attention all the time, but only to the key information they want to extract.

The attention mechanism can be implemented in various ways, such as convolutional operations and image enhancement, to automatically filter the interesting part of the information. In deep neural networks, the

Figure 7.2 Episodic personality analysis of web traits of concern [5].

attention mechanism is generally implemented by boosting the weights of regions of interest or the weights of more information-rich feature channels. Fig. 7.2 shows the feature map of spatial features extracted by the network for a single video frame in the apparent personality analysis task [5,6]. It can be seen that similar to the regions that people focus on when judging the personalities of others, networks also pay more attention to the facial expressions and hand-body movements of people.

Although the attention mechanism helps to highlight some key regions, similar to human attention, focusing on too many regions in an image can reduce the usefulness of attention and also lead to problems such as large models and slow computation. Therefore the criteria for using attention mechanisms to focus on key regions of an image are efficiency and accuracy. The following will briefly introduce a few approaches to using attentional ideas in the field of gesture recognition.

7.2 Attention mechanism as preprocess for gesture recognition

7.2.1 Light balance

During the gesture recognition process, there are many factors that affect the final result, such as lighting, background, skin color, clarity, etc. The dataset acquisition process simulates these factors to some extent that may be present in a realistic scene. Therefore, reducing the impact of these variables on the network enables the network to focus on the gesture itself. In this section, two methods for preprocessing the raw data prior to gesture recognition are presented, both of which enhance attention to the relevant part of the gesture from two perspectives: balancing the illumination of the whole video and extracting the hand region in the video.

In gesture recognition tasks, especially in dynamic gesture recognition tasks, many extraneous factors can affect the final result of gesture recognition. Illumination is one of these factors. On the one hand, the instability of illumination can lead to an increase in gesture image noise, and on the other hand, ambient light has the potential to affect the quality of the image, making it difficult for gesture features to stand out from other background features due to the small contrast between the observed gesture features and the image background features that need to be ignored. Therefore the attention mechanism can eliminate the illumination difference by preprocessing the input data to prevent the network from learning this as a variation feature. Miao et al. [7] used the Retinex image enhancement theory to reduce the effect of illumination unevenness on gesture recognition. The Retinex theory was originally proposed by Land and McCann [8] and has been widely applied to various image enhancement The theory assumes that the color of an object is inherently consistent and does not change due to differences in illumination, that is, the color is constant. As Fig. 7.3 shows, according to Retinex theory, the observed brightness of an object is determined by the combined effect of the reflected light from its surface and the incident light intensity from the external environment:

$$I(x) = L(x) \times R(x) \tag{7.1}$$

where x is the location of the pixel, $I(x)$ is the brightness of the object entering the human eye or the imaging device, that is the brightness of the image at x; $R(x)$ is the light intensity of the reflected light of the object; and $L(x)$ is the intensity of the incident light. The core idea of Retinex is to eliminate the effect of the incident light by certain means, so that the light intensity of the reflected light, which reflects the properties of the object itself, is retained. Thus the reflected light of the object can be recovered by the following equation:

$$R(x) = e^{\log I(x) - \log L(x)} \tag{7.2}$$

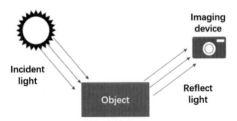

Figure 7.3 Schematic diagram of Retinex theory.

Figure 7.4 Video enhancement by Retinex [7]. (A) Raw videos in IsoGD. (B) Videos in IsoGD enhanced by Retinex.

Since the ambient light intensity of $L(x)$ is difficult to obtain directly, it is usually obtained indirectly by filtering $I(x)$ with a low-pass filter.

From Fig. 7.4A, the same gesture has different visual effects due to the difference in illumination. The dark environment makes it difficult to recognize some detailed features in the video and the effect of light and shadow makes it difficult to distinguish the human movements from the background, thus increasing the difficulty of gesture recognition. The enhancement results obtained by Retinex are shown in Fig. 7.4B. By this method, the effect of different ambient light on the video can be eliminated, and more consistent and clearer video data can be obtained, thus helping the subsequent gesture recognition network to better focus on the gesture itself and avoid the influence of irrelevant factors on gesture recognition.

7.2.2 Prehand detection

For hand gesture recognition, the position, movement, and state of the hand are the parts of the whole task that should be focused on, whether it is the human eye or a computer vision algorithm. Although there are many traditional methods that use manual features for hand information extraction, the methods rely on a lot of prior knowledge, mostly based on the characteristics of some special scenes, and once the scenes are changed, this prior knowledge also fails. Moreover it is still a great challenge to find a general precedent. Therefore some researchers [4,9,10] try to achieve the extraction of hand regions in videos by hand detection and use this as an input to assist the gesture recognition network to focus on the features of the gestures themselves.

In the process of hand detection, two commonly used algorithms are the YOLO algorithm [11−14], one of the representative works of the one-stage algorithm, and the Faster R-CNN algorithm [15], one of the representative works of the two-stage algorithm. The single-stage algorithm is an algorithm that directly estimates the class and location coordinates of the detected object, while the two-stage algorithm is a series of candidate frames (proposals), which are then filtered by convolutional neural networks (CNNs) to obtain the final target location. Both methods have their advantages and disadvantages. Generally speaking, the single-stage algorithm is faster and the two-stage algorithm is more accurate. The following section focuses on these two algorithms and the subsequent detection network, focusing on the hand region by hand detection assistance.

As mentioned earlier, the YOLO family of algorithms is a type of single-stage algorithm. The most original YOLO algorithm [11] uses a direct regression method to obtain the coordinates and target class probabilities of the current target to be detected. In 2017, Redmon et al. improved it and proposed a new version YOLO9000 [12] that can perform real-time detection of up to 9000 types of objects. Subsequently, the YOLO family of algorithms continued to evolve and grow, with the successive releases of YOLOv3 [13] and YOLOv4 [14,16]. The core point of the YOLO algorithm is that it uses the input image to predict the location and class of multiple bounding boxes simultaneously, which is an end-to-end algorithm that does not require a complex design process and uses the whole image to train the model directly, that is, it can better distinguish between the target and background areas.

Redmon et al. used YOLOv3 for hand detection, which we did in our engineering practice [13]. YOLOv3 is optimized in the backbone network compared with YOLOv1 and YOLOv2. Compared with YOLOv1 and YOLOv2, YOLOv3 has been optimized in the backbone network. The framework structure of YOLOv3 is shown in Fig. 7.5, and its structure is similar to that of ResNet [17]. When using YOLOv3 for prediction, the video frames fed into the network are normalized by scale, and subsequently, features are extracted by the backbone network. For objects of different scales, the output is divided into three. The multiscale prediction method is used to extract features from several feature maps of different scales to improve the adaptability of the network to objects of different sizes. In terms of the loss function, YOLOv3 adopts the binary cross-entropy loss function instead of the original Softmax loss function.

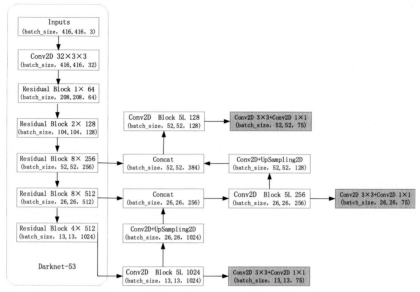

Figure 7.5 YOLOv3 framework diagram.

Overall, YOLOv3 is faster and more accurate than the YOLOv1 and YOLOv2 algorithms.

In the detection phase, the Oxford hand dataset [18] is used to train the YOLOv3 hand detector, and the trained detector performs hand detection for each frame in the dynamic video. The obtained hand images are used as input for the recognition phase. In the subsequent recognition stage, the hand images framed by the detector are extracted for spatial features using a 2D CNN. The extracted features consider only the spatial features of the hand region, which can effectively reduce the negative effects of gesture-independent factors (e.g., background, clothing, body, etc.). Fig. 7.6 demonstrates the effect of YOLOv3 in detecting hand regions.

Faster R-CNN [15] is another commonly used detector. This detector improves on the R-CNN [19] and Fast R-CNN [20] to further enhance the speed. The detector is divided into two parts: the candidate bounding box is extracted by constructing the region proposal network (RPN) to complete the candidate target coarse localization. Then the coarse localization region obtained from the RPN network is further refined in the subsequent network, and the final bounding box is filtered by further learning, while the location and class of the target are predicted.

Figure 7.6 YOLOv3 hand detection effect.

Liu et al. [10] applied faster R–CNN to a dynamic continuous gesture recognition task. The application of the detector can be divided into two parts. The first part is shown in Fig. 7.7. Similar to the author's idea of detecting hand regions using YOLOv3, Liu et al. also detect hand and face regions from each frame (where only localization points are kept in the face region instead of the whole face) and then remove other regions to eliminate the interference of other gesture-independent factors on the results. Liu et al. then used 3D convolution kernels to extract features to focus on the time-domain variation features of the hand.

In the second part, for the continuous gesture recognition problem, Liu et al. used hand detection for the segmentation of continuous gestures. In the commonly used continuous gesture dataset, ConGD (which is also a continuous gesture subset of the CGD dataset), the performers in each video put their hands back to the original state after making a gesture and then start the next gesture. Based on this phenomenon, Liu et al. analyzed the position of the hand detection frame to determine whether the frame is in the interval between two gestures or the process of gesture performance. Specifically, as shown in Fig. 7.8, they assumed

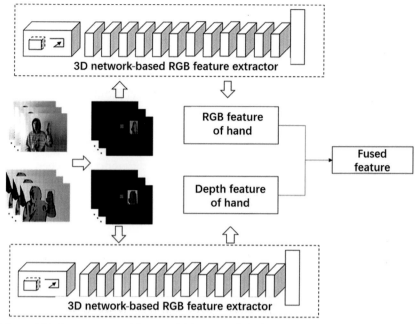

Figure 7.7 Gesture recognition model framework [10].

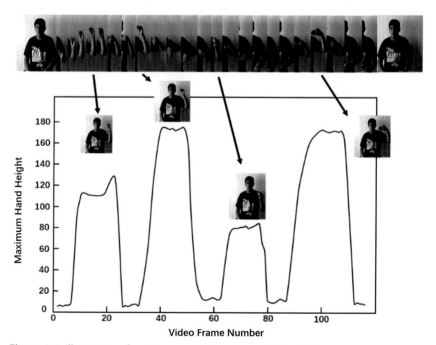

Figure 7.8 Illustration of continuous gesture segmentation [10].

that when either hand appears above the set threshold, it indicates the beginning of a new gesture. If both hands are below the set threshold at the same time, it indicates the end of the gesture. Using the above segmentation strategy, they converted the continuous gesture recognition problem into a relatively simple independent gesture recognition problem. The subsequent recognition is performed according to the framework shown in Fig. 7.7.

To summarize the above examples, when using hand detection to assist in the implementation of gesture recognition, the following different treatments can be carried out according to the differences between static and dynamic gesture recognition:

In static gesture recognition, since there is no temporal dimension, the recognition process usually focuses only on the spatial location of the hand, and the training model needs to be trained only on the hand. In practical applications, a hand image is framed using a detection model, and then a classification model is trained to perform gesture recognition from the hand-only image data.

In dynamic gesture recognition, hand information cannot fully represent a gesture because dynamic gestures are also related to information such as the direction of arm movement and the motion process. In this case, the extracted local features of the hand can be used as a complement to the global video features [21] to highlight the spatial location of the hand region in each frame, thus enhancing the network's focus on hand movement changes in general.

7.3 Attention mechanism based on complementarity of different modal data

The attention mechanisms mentioned in Section 7.2 are adjusted overall or locally. For example, light balancing is used to reduce the impact of light changes on gesture recognition from the overall image, while hand predetection is used to extract more information from the local area. In fact, due to the complementary nature of different modalities, different modal data can also be used as an aid to help the network focus on gesture-related regions of the video and avoid the interference of irrelevant information. In this section, methods to eliminate the interference of gesture irrelevant factors using skeletal data, saliency data, and optical flow data are presented.

7.3.1 Attention mechanism based on skeletal data

In gesture recognition, the utilization of skeletal data is similar to hand detectors in that they can both be used to eliminate the influence of gesture-independent factors such as background and clothing on recognition accuracy. In static gesture recognition, the use of skeletal data often requires a clear image of the hand or accurate skeletal key points of the hand to generate the corresponding keypoint map. Dynamic gesture recognition not only focuses on hand information but also on torso information. As such dynamic gesture recognition can often draw on skeleton extraction methods to enhance the focus on torso information.

Thus dynamic gesture recognition utilizes skeletal data as a complement to other modal data. Because the bones not only provide effective spatial information, the joint information of the bones can also assist in processing the RGB data input, making the model more focused on the changing part of the hand.

As shown in Fig. 7.9, Baradel et al. [22] proposed a multimodal dual-stream fusion model for gesture recognition by fusing skeletal data with raw RGB data. In this context, the skeletal branch input is not just keypoint coordinates, but a three-channel vector after encoding: the first channel corresponds to the (x, y, z) coordinates of each original joint point, the second channel corresponds to the first-order derivative of the coordinates (i.e., velocity), and the third channel corresponds to the second-order derivative of the coordinates (i.e., acceleration). In the network of Baradel et al. the skeletal data are input to the network as a separate modality on the one hand, and as an adjunct to the RGB data to construct a spatiotemporal attention model on the other. In the spatial domain, they construct a spatial attention model by highlighting the hand movements and their associated items in the RGB data with the aid of the nodal information of the wrist part in the skeletal data. This is because many actions, such as reading, writing, drinking, etc., are relatively similar in hand shape and need to be judged according to the items held to determine the category of the action. In the temporal domain, they input the combination of different modal data into the LSTM network to construct a temporal attention model and then extract features. This design can improve the accuracy of recognition by focusing more on the focus of the action, that is, the information of hand details.

Another feasible approach is to generate a heatmap of the corresponding region from skeletal data to guide the recognition network to focus on the spatial location of the hand. Zhou et al. [23] generated a heatmap by

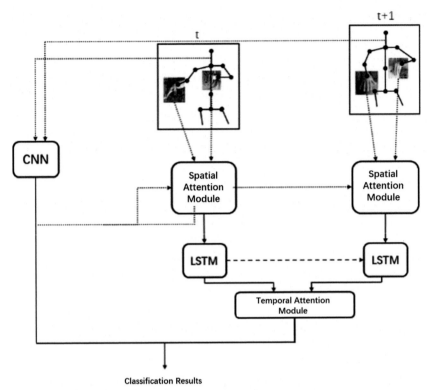

Figure 7.9 Multimodal dual-flow model proposed by Baradel et al. [22].

Gaussian convolution of skeletal data to highlight the location of the hand, arm, and other parts in the image and learned the regionalized feature by constructing HeatmapNet and using it as a salient feature to assist network learning. As shown in Fig. 7.10, Zhou et al. generated the corresponding skeletal data for each frame of RGB data, and then performed Gaussian convolution on the skeletal keypoint data. Since there are more keypoints in the hand region, the Gaussians of the hand keypoints can be superimposed by such a method to highlight the hand region.

Based on this, Zhou et al. used the generated heatmap as a supervised image for hand region attention, as shown in Fig. 7.11. The HeatmapNet, as shown in Fig. 7.11, learns such highlighted hand features and divides the learned features into multiple scales according to the scale of the features in the main network, namely the gesture recognition learning network. It then feeds them into the main network layer by layer, and assigns a higher weight to the corresponding region of each layer of features, to enhance the network's attention to the hand region.

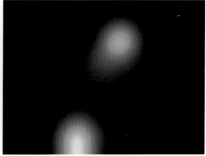

Figure 7.10 Static saliency attention.

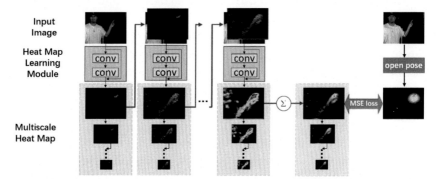

Figure 7.11 Network structure of HeatmapNet in the method of Zhou et al. [23]. *Copyright © 2024, Association for the Advancement of Artificial Intelligence. Citation to the original publication is required. All rights reserved should appear beneath figures, and permission to reuse figures for other purposes (or granting it to others) is NOT allowed.*

Some scholars directly use skeletal data for gesture recognition instead of using it as an aid to RGB data [24,25]. This approach is generally combined with the graph neural network to construct a graph model using the association information between the joint points of skeletal data, which provides a new idea for gesture and action recognition.

7.3.1.1 Attention mechanism based on salient features

As we mentioned in Chapter 6, human visual saliency regions are selected as the salient regions in natural images that best attract human attention according to the human visual attention mechanism, so saliency itself is a manifestation of the attention mechanism. The introduction of saliency allows the network to better focus on regions related to gestures and avoid interference from background and other variables unrelated to gestures.

Li et al. [26] extracted RGB features and saliency features separately by the C3D model and fused them to obtain the final prediction results. In this method, saliency data is generated from RGB data according to the method in the literature [27], which focuses on the salient object in the video, that is, the performer's body, and helps to eliminate the influence of background and clothes, which can be considered as an aid to RGB data. Together with depth data, the three are fused to enhance the final recognition performance by taking advantage of their complementary nature. Fig. 7.12 shows the gesture recognition network framework designed by Li et al.

7.3.1.2 Attention mechanism based on optical flow characteristics

In dynamic gesture recognition tasks, the change in hand motion is crucial and the motion information allows the computer to understand the time-domain information of the gesture. Optical flow is a method used to describe the change in motion of an object in a scene between two consecutive frames due to its own motion or camera motion. Therefore, the introduction of optical flow is extremely helpful for gesture recognition.

The study by Simonyan and Zisserman [28] is an early method to obtain action change information from optical flow data. As shown in Fig. 7.13, Simonyan and Zisserman extracted the spatial information from

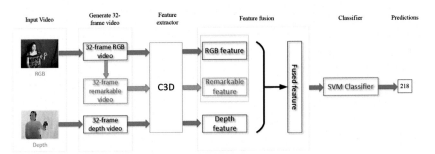

Figure 7.12 Network framework of Li et al. [26].

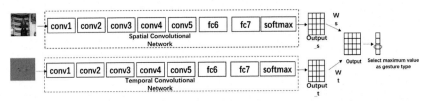

Figure 7.13 Simonyan and Zisserman network structure diagram.

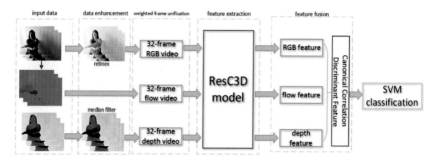

Figure 7.14 Network structure diagram of Li et al. [29].

RGB data using a 2D CNN, and focused on the motion information by extracting the features of optical flow data through a 2D CNN, and then fused the two features to form the spatiotemporal information for action classification.

In addition to this, Li et al. [29] used optical flow techniques to eliminate the influence of factors, such as video background in RGB data, to avoid factors unrelated to gestures from affecting recognition results. As shown in Fig. 7.14, Miao et al. [26] used the saliency modality method based on optical flow data and RGB data as the two input streams of the C3D model. After extracting the features, the final classification results are obtained by fusing them.

In gesture recognition, RGB data focuses on the overall spatial information. Skeletal data focuses on the most essential movement change information. Saliency data focuses on the salient region in the video, usually the body part of the action performer, and optical flow data focuses on the motion information between two frames, with each modality having its own focus. By exploiting the complementarity between multiple modalities, it can further complement the information that cannot be attended to by individual modal data, thus helping the network to focus its attention on the gesture action itself and learn a better feature representation. However, the attention mechanism can be computationally intensive and should be used with a reasonable design to strike a balance between computational accuracy and complexity.

7.4 Summary

Attention mechanisms originate from the study of human processes of observing things. In cognitive science, since a large amount of information cannot be processed in real time and with equal weight, humans selectively focus on some of the information and ignore others of little value. In the field of computer vision, attention mechanisms are usually introduced to highlight regions of an image or video that are more relevant to the task. This mechanism enables automatic filtering of task-relevant information. This chapter introduces several attention methods for gesture recognition, including methods based on preprocessing and methods that exploit the complementarity of different modal data to implement attention mechanisms.

References

[1] V. Mnih, N. Heess, A. Graves, Recurrent models of visual attention, in: Proceedings on Advances in Neural Information Processing Systems, 2014, pp. 2204–2212.

[2] A. Vaswani, N. Shazeer, N. Parmar, et al., Attention is all you need, in: Proceedings on Advances in Neural Information Processing Systems, 2017, pp. 1–11.

[3] W.J. Li, Traffic Command Gesture Recognition Based on Skeletonization and Template Matching, Zhejiang University of Technology, Zhejiang, 2011.

[4] H. Wang, P. Wang, Z. Song, et al., Large-scale multimodal gesture recognition using heterogeneous networks, in: Proceedings of IEEE International Conference on Computer Vision Workshops, 2017, pp. 3129–3137.

[5] Y. Li, J. Wan, Q. Miao, et al., CR-Net: a deep classification-regression network for multimodal apparent personality analysis, International Journal of Computer Vision (2020) 1–18.

[6] H.J. Escalante, H. Kaya, A.A. Salah, et al., Explaining first impressions: modeling, recognizing, and explaining apparent personality from videos, arXiv preprint arXiv 00745 (1802) 2018.

[7] Q. Miao, Y. Li, W. Ouyang, et al., Multimodal gesture recognition based on the RESC3D network, in: Proceedings of IEEE International Conference on Computer Vision Workshops, 2017, pp. 3047–3055.

[8] E.H. Land, J.J. McCann, Lightness and retinex theory, JOSA 61 (1) (1971) 1–11.

[9] X. Chai, Z. Liu, F. Yin, et al., Two streams recurrent neural networks for large-scale continuous gesture recognition, in: Proceedings IEEE, 2016, pp. 31–36.

[10] Z. Liu, X. Chai, Z. Liu, et al., Continuous gesture recognition with hand-oriented spatiotemporal feature, in: Proceedings of IEEE International Conference on Computer Vision Workshops, 2017, pp. 3056–3064.

[11] J. Redmon, S. Divvala, R. Girshick, et al., You only look once: unified, real-time object detection, in: Proceedings of IEEE Conference on Computer Vision and Pattern Recognition, 2016, pp. 779–788.

[12] J. Redmon, A. Farhadi, YOLO9000: better, faster, stronger, in: Proceedings of IEEE Conference on Computer Vision and Pattern Recognition, 2017, pp. 7263–7271.

[13] J. Redmon, A. Farhadi, Yolov3: an incremental improvement, arXiv preprint arXiv 02767 (1804) 2018.

[14] A. Bochkovskiy, C.Y. Wang, H.Y.M. Liao, Yolov4: optimal speed and accuracy of object detection, arXiv preprint arXiv 10934 (2004) 2020.

[15] S. Ren, K. He, R. Girshick, et al., Faster R-CNN: towards real-time object detection with region proposal networks, arXiv preprint arXiv 1506 (2015) 01497.

[16] Ultralytics, Yolov5 [EB/OL]. <https://github.com/ultralytics/yolov5>, 2021.

[17] K. He, X. Zhang, S. Ren et al., Deep residual learning for image recognition, in: Proceedings of IEEE Conference on Computer Vision and Pattern Recognition, 2016, pp. 770−778.

[18] A. Mittal, A. Zisserman, P.H.S. Torr, Hand detection using multiple proposals, in: Proceedings of British Machine Vision Conference, 2011, pp. 1−11.

[19] R. Girshick, J. Donahue, T. Darrell, et al., Rich feature hierarchies for accurate object detection and semantic segmentation, in: Proceedings of IEEE Conference on Computer Vision and Pattern Recognition, 2014, pp. 580−587.

[20] R. Girshick, Fast R-CNN, in: Proceedings of IEEE International Conference on Computer Vision, 2015, pp. 1440−1448.

[21] Z. Liang, Z. Guangming, M. Lin, et al., Attention in convolutional LSTM for gesture recognition, in: Proceedings on Advances in Neural Information Processing Systems, 2018, pp. 1953−1962.

[22] F. Baradel, C. Wolf, J. Mille, Pose-conditioned spatio-temporal attention for human action recognition, arXiv preprint arXiv 10106 (1703) 2017.

[23] B. Zhou, Y. Li, J. Wan, Regional attention with architecture-rebuilt 3D network for RGB-D gesture recognition, in: Proceedings of annual AAAI Conference on Artificial Intelligence, 2021.

[24] J. Hou, G. Wang, X. Chen, et al., Spatial-temporal attention res-TCN for skeleton-based dynamic hand gesture recognition, in: Proceedings of European Conference on Computer Vision Workshops, 2018.

[25] Q. De Smedt, H. Wannous, J.P. Vandeborre, Skeleton-based dynamic hand gesture recognition, in: Proceedings of IEEE Conference on Computer Vision and Pattern Recognition Workshops, 2016, pp. 1−9.

[26] Y. Li, Q. Miao, K. Tian, et al., Large-scale gesture recognition with a fusion of RGB-D data based on saliency theory and C3D model, IEEE Transactions on Circuits and Systems for Video Technology 28 (10) (2018) 2956−2964.

[27] R. Achanta, F. Estrada, P. Wils, et al., Salient region detection and segmentation, in: Proceedings of International Conference on Computer Vision Systems, Springer, 2008, pp. 66−75.

[28] K. Simonyan, A. Zisserman, Two-stream convolutional networks for action recognition in videos, in: Proceedings on Advances in Neural Information Processing Systems, 2014, pp. 1−9.

[29] Y. Li, Q. Miao, K. Tian, et al., Large-scale gesture recognition with a fusion of RGB-D data based on optical flow and the C3D model, Pattern Recognition Letters 119 (2019) 187−194.

CHAPTER 8

Gesture recognition-based human−computer interaction cases

8.1 Application areas of gesture recognition

As an important part of human−computer interaction, the development of gesture recognition affects the naturalness and flexibility of human−computer interaction. Gesture recognition has a wide range of application areas as the development direction of new human−computer interaction modes.

8.1.1 Intelligent driving

It is well known that there are certain unsafe factors in the interaction between automobile drivers and automobile control devices during driving, mainly because drivers may be distracted from driving in the process of human−computer interaction with automobiles. Currently, in-vehicle human−computer interaction is mainly carried out through touch displays and voice. Although the touch precision and response speed of the touch display have been continuously improved, the fact that touch control must rely on the user's contact with the screen surface limits the user's operating space and flexibility. In terms of voice recognition, although the relevant technologies and products are more mature, voice recognition still has limitations in handling persistent commands, such as adjusting the volume of the stereo and the progress of music [1]. As shown in Fig. 8.1, the flexibility of gesture recognition can better complement the above two technologies. Therefore, a multilevel interaction mode that integrates touch, voice, and gesture control is gradually being focused on by automakers.

8.1.2 Smart home control

As shown in Fig. 8.2, smart home control systems are known by many names, including smart home, home automation, and integrated home systems. Of these names, smart home is the more familiar one. The system generally uses the home as a platform to integrate technologies such as integrated wiring,

Gesture Recognition
DOI: https://doi.org/10.1016/B978-0-443-28959-0.00006-6

Figure 8.1 Example of gesture recognition in intelligent driving.

Figure 8.2 Example of gesture recognition in smart home control.

network communications, security, and automation. The purpose is to provide convenient control of home electronics, including audio, video, home office, telecommunications, security, lighting, air conditioning, and more.

Smart homes can make residents' lives easier and safer than traditional homes. Whether residents are at work or on vacation, the smart home will remind residents of emergencies at home. The smart home system can automatically regulate the power consumption of some household equipment, transitioning them into the sleep state when idle. In the event of a wake-up state, it aims to achieve the effective use of energy. In addition, for the elderly living alone and disabled people with limited mobility, the smart home can provide real-time health monitoring, and in the event of an accident, it can also send timely notifications to medical institutions and relatives. This undoubtedly provides greater convenience for residents.

In a smart home, human—computer interaction is an important part. Compared with the traditional human—computer interaction mode, the contactless human—computer interaction realized using gesture recognition is more flexible and natural. It allows users to control various smart home appliances anywhere in the home using only gesture movements. For example, users can turn on and off the lights in a room, adjust the volume of a TV, or adjust the temperature of a refrigerator with simple customized gestures without using a remote control. This is undoubtedly an important development direction for the smart home.

8.1.3 Unmanned aerial vehicle control

A drone, or unmanned aerial vehicle (UAV), is a vehicle that is controlled by an onboard flight computer or a handheld remote-control device. While the development of UAVs was first driven by military applications, in recent years, a variety of technological advances have led to the development of a low-cost civilian solution for nonmilitary applications. We are seeing an increasing number of small UAVs designed for use in livelihood applications such as photogrammetry, remote sensing, forestry and agriculture, environment, and energy [2].

Conventional UAV control is generally carried out via a remote control, where the user sends operational commands to the UAV via joysticks and buttons on the remote control. This traditional control method can communicate with the drone over long distances and can be adapted to a wide range of flight tasks in different environments. However, the disadvantage is that it has higher requirements for operators, who need to learn a series of usage methods and operation commands. With the development of gesture recognition technology, combining gesture recognition with UAV control has undoubtedly become a new mode of UAV control. As shown in Fig. 8.3, with gesture recognition technology, the user does not need to learn professional operating instructions and can control the flight of the UAV only through user-defined gesture movements. This new model of drone control better meets the needs of the general public for drone use.

8.1.4 Robot control

With the development of robotics technology, robots have gradually entered people's daily life from the experimental samples in the laboratory

Figure 8.3 Example of gesture recognition in UAV control. *UAV,* Unmanned aerial vehicle.

in the beginning. Robots have been able to replace human beings to do part of the work in factories, and also provide entertainment and help to people in their daily life. As a result, interactions between humans and robots have become more and more frequent. The traditional human–robot interaction technology based on mouse and keyboard has the disadvantage of being mechanized and not easy to grasp, which can no longer meet the needs of people interacting with robots. Human–robot interaction technology needs to develop in the direction of simplicity and humanization. Gesture, as a common way of communication between people, contains more information and has the advantages of naturalness, simplicity, and directness. Therefore the importance of the robot control mode based on gesture recognition has become more and more prominent (Fig. 8.4).

8.2 Gesture recognition case studies

8.2.1 Gesture recognition case 1: drone control

This case aims to realize the flight control of the UAV using static hand gestures by using a visible light camera mounted on the UAV. Depending on the recognition results for different hands, the UAV can be controlled in flight directions such as ascending, descending, panning, hovering, etc. (as shown in Fig. 8.5). In addition, other expandable functions of the UAV besides flight are considered. Therefore gesture control is also realized for auxiliary functions equipped on the UAV, such as taking pictures and videos.

Figure 8.4 Gesture in robot control.

Figure 8.5 Demonstration of drone gesture control.

The flowchart of the case is shown in Fig. 8.6. It can be mainly divided into three important stages: face detection, hand detection, and gesture recognition.

In the scene captured by the camera carried by the UAV, factors such as the height of the UAV flight, the distance from the operator, and the relative angle to the operator are taken into account. The operator may not be present in the captured scene, or there may be some scenes that are not related to the gesture movement, such as stacked debris, passing vehicles, and complex vistas. It is undoubtedly very difficult and costly to directly perform gesture movement recognition in such complex situations. Therefore to determine the presence of the operator in the image and to be able to better localize the location of the operator, it is necessary

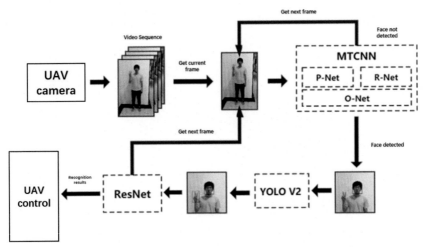

Figure 8.6 The flowchart of gesture recognition in our UAV control project. *UAV,* Unmanned aerial vehicle.

to perform a face detection operation on the captured video data. This step provides a good basis for subsequent recognition.

Face detection, an important research topic in the field of computer vision, has produced very rich research results under the drilling of many researchers. Among them MTCNN (multitask convolutional neural network) is the most commonly used target detection network in this field [3]. MTCNN consists of three subconvolutional networks called P-Net, R-Net, and R-Net. The input image is changed into different scales by constructing an image pyramid model. The input images of different scales will be fed into the three subnetworks, P-Net, R-Net, and R-Net, and the detected face regions and keypoints of the face are generated by the nonmaximum suppression algorithm and the bounding box regression algorithm. There are five generated face keypoints located in the left eye, right eye, nose, left corner of the mouth, and right corner of the mouth, and the detection process is as follows. MTCNN has good performance in terms of speed and accuracy of face detection compared with other methods. Considering that we need to detect faces in the video under real-time conditions, means that the detection process requires less time, less overhead, and higher accuracy. Therefore the two advantages of MTCNN are just enough to fulfill our needs.

Since MTCNN is a still image-based face detection method, the video captured by the UAV needs to be processed as a continuous sequence of images, that is, each image in the image sequence represents each frame in the video. For each frame, MTCNN is applied to detect the face region and face keypoints. If the presence of a face is detected in the current frame, then it goes to the next stage, and if the face is not detected in the current frame, then the next frame is input. The flow of this part is shown in Fig. 8.7.

8.2.1.1 Hand detection

After the face detection stage, if there is a face in the current image, then it can be assumed that there is a drone operator in the image. The face region output by face detection can determine the position of the

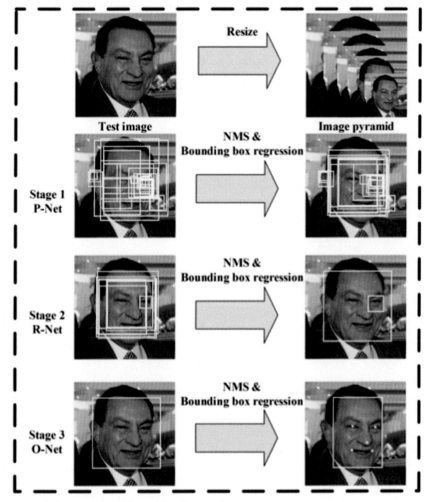

Figure 8.7 Flowchart of face detection section.

operator located in the image. Based on this we can do further processing of the image.

The region where the hand is located in the image is very important when performing gesture action recognition. However, in the image captured by the camera, the region of the operator's hand is a very small percentage of the whole scene. This means that it is difficult to detect the position of the hand and recognize the gesture directly in the whole image because other irrelevant factors in the image can easily affect the detection and recognition results. Taking this into account, it is necessary to estimate the region of the operator's hand within which the recognition can be performed to improve the reliability of the recognition results.

As a rule of thumb, a UAV operator performing gesture movements to a flying UAV generally needs to raise his or her arms for the demonstration of the movements. Then, a certain geometric relationship will be formed between the raised hand and the operator's face. Relying on this a priori knowledge and the face region output from the face detection step, we can estimate the approximate region where the operator's hand exists. Part of the code for hand region estimation is shown below:

```
double width_factor = 2.2;
int x = static_cast<int>(itr->x - itr->width * width_factor);
x = x < 0 ? 0 : x;
double height_factor = 1.8
int y = static_cast<int>(itr->y - itr->height / height_factor);
y = y < 0 ? 0 : y;

int width = static_cast<int>(width_factor * itr->width);
width = (x + width) < img->col? width : img->cols - x;
int height = static_cast<int>(2.1 * itr->height);
height = (y + height) < img->rows ? height : img->rows - y;

itr->x = x;
itr->width = width;
itr->y = y;
itr->height = height;
```

where   itr->x,   itr->y,   itr->width,   itr->height   denote   the x-coordinate and y-coordinate of the upper-left vertex of the face region (rectangular region) output by the face detection as well as the width and height of the face region, respectively. Lines 2 and 5 of the code indicate that the x-coordinate and y-coordinate of the face are shifted to the upper left of the image based on two set parameters, width_factor and height_factor, taking into account the region where the operator's gesture action may occur based on experience. Check whether the coordinates cross the boundary of the image while moving, as shown in lines 3 and 6. The x-coordinate and y-coordinate after moving represent the x-coordinate and y-coordinate of the code estimated for the upper left vertex of the hand region. The operations in lines 9 and 12 are similar to the above, where the width and height of the hand region are estimated based on the set parameters and the length and width of the face region. It is also necessary to check whether the estimated height and width exceed the maximum size of the image.

The hand region estimation limits the recognition to a smaller region compared with the original whole image. To further constrain the size of this region, more accurate hand detection operations need to be performed within this region. Considering the real-time requirements of the whole system and the constraints of the UAV itself on computing performance, the YOLO target detection algorithm, which is widely used in the field of target detection, is a suitable choice because of its fast computing speed and low background false detection rate. The YOLO V2 version we choose here is based on the original YOLO algorithm, which greatly improves accuracy and reduces the amount of computation.

The YOLO algorithm detects the hand and obtains the exact position of the hand in the estimation area. However, in practice, the operator's left and right hands may be in the estimation area at the same time. In this case, the YOLO algorithm detects multiple hand positions. Since the position of the hand that demonstrates the action is more toward the center of the estimation region, the Euclidean distance between the center of each detected hand position and the center of the estimation region is calculated, and the one with the smallest distance is selected for the final recognition process.

8.2.1.2 Gesture recognition

For the identified hand regions, the final gesture recognition phase needs to classify them into the correct category and output them. This phase is the most important because the correctness of the classification directly affects the effectiveness of the whole system.

Considering the characteristics of this case based on static gestures and the high demand for accuracy, ResNet is a good choice [4]. ResNet introduces the concept of residual learning based on the traditional convolutional network, which solves the problems of gradient disappearance and model convergence when the number of layers of the network is deepened and has achieved excellent results in the field of image classification.

Combining the computing resources, hardware platform, and other practical conditions, we finally chose ResNet18, which is more suitable for gesture recognition among the many variants of ResNet. The key codes of the network call and result output are as follows:

```
classify_desc_path = ". /models/resnet_desc.prototxt";
classify_bi_path = ". /models/resnet_iter_1000.caffemodel"
net = cv::dnn::readNetFromCaffe(classify_desc_path,
classify_bi_path);

cv::Mat dec;
cv::cvtColor(*img, dec, cv::COLOR_RGB2BGR);
cv::Mat inputBlob =cv::dnn:blobFromImage(dec, 1.0,
cv::Size(cnn_crop_sie, cnn_crop_size),
cv::Scalar()).
cv::Mat prob;
DetectorKit::get_instance()->net.setInput(inputBlob, "data");
prob = DetectorKit::get_instance()->net.forward("prob");

int classId.
double classProb.
getMaxClass(prob, &classId, &classProb);
```

As illustrated in the above pseudocode, the network model that has been trained using the Caffe deep learning platform needs to be loaded (shown in rows 1—3). For the input, hand images also need to be pre-processed in some way. As shown in rows 5—6, the color space of the image is converted from RGB to BGR color space by default in OpenCV. In addition, to meet the requirements of the network input, the overall pixel values of the image need to be subtracted from the average value, and the image size is scaled. After the preprocessing operations are performed, the image can be fed into the network, and the predictive distribution of the network for the classification result can be obtained through forward propagation (shown in lines 10—12). Since the likelihood of the gesture being classified into each category is represented in the predictive distribution of the result, the final output prediction should be the most probable of the categories (shown in lines 14—16).

The final output of the network's recognition results will be used for the control of the UAV. Based on the different kinds of gesture movements recognized and the predefined operations corresponding to the gestures, the UAV can then perform different flight maneuvers and other auxiliary functions according to the operator's gestures.

8.2.2 Gesture recognition case 2: smart home control

Smart home appliances are an important part of the smart home. The user's interaction with smart home appliances is, to some extent, the interaction with the whole smart home system. Nowadays, the more common interaction mode is based on remote control. This mode of interaction is undoubtedly more cumbersome for users, because users need to use different remote controls to control different appliances. Moreover, for different types of home appliances, users may need to learn how to use different remote controls. With the development of artificial intelligence technology and computer vision, the contactless interaction mode based on gesture control can better solve the above problems. Users only need to use different defined gestures to control all the home appliances at home, without the need to spend time and cost on learning how to use different appliances.

Based on this vision, this case focuses on dynamic gesture-based smart home appliance control system that can be deployed on a mobile platform using deep learning techniques. In the system, users can perform dynamic gesture actions through a common visible light camera, and realize real-time control of home appliances based on the meanings defined by different actions.

The flow of this system is shown in Fig. 8.8, which can be summarized into three modules based on real-time video stream acquisition, gesture segmentation, and video gesture recognition. The real-time video stream data is captured by a visible light camera as an input device, then a sliding window based gesture segmentation is utilized to obtain approximate independent gesture segments, and finally the independent gesture segments are used for dynamic gesture recognition. The output recognition results will be used to manipulate the smart home appliances to fulfill the corresponding functions.

8.2.2.1 Hardware platform

Since this system is carried out under the important condition of deep learning technology, it has certain requirements for the computing power and hardware conditions of the devices. Some home appliances have the demand for miniaturization and flexible mobility. Therefore the hardware platform used in the system should be small in size, flexible, lightweight, and have good computing performance. Therefore we consider using NVIDIA Jetson Xavier (hereinafter referred to as Xavier), a small computer system produced by NVIDIA for artificial intelligence and industrial automation, as the running platform of the whole system, which is equipped with NVIDIA's self-developed Carmel 8-core 64-bit CPUs and Volta 512-core GPUs. The Volta architecture 512-core GPU has powerful data computing and processing capabilities. The Xavier kit also provides a variety of I/O ports, such as USB, Type-C 3.1, HDMI, and Gigabit Ethernet ports. Xavier itself is only the size of the palm of our hand, which fits right in with our need for lightweight and mobility.

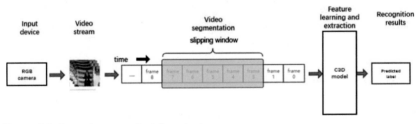

Figure 8.8 Smart home project flowchart.

8.2.2.2 Input device

Gesture control-based home appliance interaction generally requires the use of cameras for image or video data capture. Cameras can be categorized into visible light cameras, infrared cameras, depth cameras, and so on, depending on the modality of the captured data. However, infrared cameras and depth cameras have the disadvantages of high cost and are difficult to use in practice. The common visible light camera is low cost, easy to carry and move, and easy to integrate with smart home appliances, so it is used as an input device for video data acquisition.

In addition, to be able to better process the data captured by the visible light camera, the use of OpenCV as a support is considered, which is an open-source, cross-platform computer vision library that can run on a variety of platforms rated operating systems. It is lightweight and efficient, provides rich interfaces for multiple programming languages, and is widely used in image processing.

8.2.2.3 Construction of dataset

In deep learning-based methods, it is very important to construct a suitable dataset. A reasonable dataset can make the network model better adapted to the actual use of the environment and can work efficiently and stably in the face of a variety of complex situations.

When constructing the dataset used for this project, taking the interaction between the user and the smart TV set as an example, the training data and test data are all collected under normal indoor lighting conditions to simulate the lighting environment that the user is exposed to at home on a daily basis. Considering that the distance between the user and the TV is usually 2—4 m, we also keep the distance between the performer and the camera within this range when shooting the data set. While watching TV, the user may be in a sitting or standing position, so we require the performers to complete the specified actions in standing and sitting positions. In practice, the difference in the scenery around the user may affect the stability of the recognition results, so it is necessary to include the change in background in the dataset. Therefore we consider two background environments when shooting the dataset, one is a simple background, that is, the background is clean and free of clutter, such as a white wall, and the other is a complex background, that is, there are more irrelevant objects in the background, such as books on the bookshelf that are cluttered with visiting books.

Under the above conditions, we have separately captured a wide range of gesture actions that may be required when users interact with the TV. The meanings of the gesture actions include turning on and off the TV, increasing and decreasing the volume of the TV, and fast forwarding and rewinding the TV program. During the performance of gesture movements, it is required that the movement lasts about 4 seconds from the beginning to the end, and the whole process is uniform and stable. Taking the three gesture actions of clapping, waving, and snapping fingers (shown in Fig. 8.9) in the dataset as an example, we define the meanings of these three gestures in the actual interaction as the three commonly used operations of turning on the TV set, fast-forwarding of the current program, and turning off the TV set.

Applause, the opening movement of television, requires two hands to strike each other, and when the performer is in a standing position, both hands are naturally down at the start. When the action is performed, both hands are placed in front of the chest, and the palm of the right hand is lightly struck against the palm of the left hand, usually repeated two to four times, with both hands naturally placed on the side of the leg after completion. When the performer is in a seated position, the hands are placed naturally on the legs at the start, and the hands are placed in front of the chest when clapping. The same is repeated two to four times, using the right palm to tap the left palm, returning the hands to the starting position when the movement is complete.

Figure 8.9 Schematic diagram of clapping, waving, and finger-snapping motions.

The waving movement is the fast-forward operation of the current program that requires waving the arms according to a certain trajectory of the performer. When the performer is in a standing position, the hands are naturally lowered at the beginning, the right hand is waved from right to left at a constant speed during the execution of the movement, and the right hand is naturally lowered after the completion of the movement. When the performer is in a seated position, the hands are placed naturally on the legs, the right hand swings from right to left at a constant speed, and the hands are restored to the starting position after the completion of the movement.

The finger-snapping action, that is, the turning off of a television set, requires the performer to use the middle finger of the right hand to strike the thumb area while the arm is swung from top to bottom. Since only video data collection is performed, this maneuver does not require the performer's finger-snapping action to necessarily make a sound. When the performer is standing, the starting position is with both hands hanging down naturally; the right hand is placed in front of the chest for one finger strike; the right arm is swung slightly downward; and both hands are lowered after the finger strike. When the performer is in a sitting position, both hands are naturally placed on the legs at the beginning, and the requirements for finger snapping are similar to those in a standing position, with both hands restored to the starting position after completion.

In the final dataset obtained from the collection, we used 70% of the samples for training the model and 15% for validation. The last 15% of the samples are used to evaluate the accuracy of the model in the condition where the input is a full gesture action.

8.2.2.4 Video streaming data acquisition module

Considering the real-time environment in which smart home appliances are used, this project uses video stream data captured from an ordinary visible light camera as input. The currently used visible light camera captures three-channel RGB video with a resolution of 640×480 and a frame rate of 30 frames/second. This stage requires the ability to capture video streaming data in a stable and continuous manner and to be able to write to a standard format video file when required.

8.2.2.5 Gesture segmentation module

If gesture recognition is required in a continuous video stream, it is necessary to determine the boundary positions of neighboring gesture actions to segment the continuous video stream into independent gesture segments. To realize the segmentation function of consecutive gesture actions while meeting the computation time requirement, we adopt an approximate gesture segmentation method here. This method creates a buffer of fixed-length video sequences, that is, a sliding window, which slides along the video stream in a certain step size, and performs feature extraction and classification of the video frame sequences within the window after each slide. As per the assumption, the duration of a gesture action is 4 seconds. Meanwhile, since the deep neural network model used in this scheme requires the input to be a frame sequence of length 16. Therefore, the length of the sliding window is set to 16, and for the acquired video streaming data of 30 frames per second, 4 frames need to be sampled equidistant within one second, that is, 1 frame at an interval of 8 frames. The sampled frames are added to the end of the sliding window, while the 4 frames at the front of the window are discarded. Each time the above operation is completed, the sliding window is considered to have slid once, and the general flow is shown in Fig. 8.10.

Under the premise of cooperative sampling, approximate segmentation can be realized for video streams with fixed individual gesture lengths to obtain complete gesture video segments, which contain the complete flow of predesigned actions from start to finish. The key code for this segment is shown below:

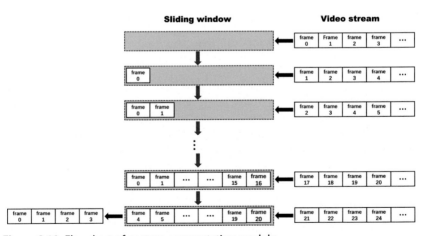

Figure 8.10 Flowchart of gesture segmentation module.

```
vector<cv::Mat> frameArray;
cv::VideoCapture capture(0);
if (!capture.isOpened()){
  cout << "can not ope capture" << endl;
  return -1;
}
int frameRate = capture.get(CV_CAP_PROP_FPS);
while (capture.isOpened()){
  for (int i = 0; i < framerate; ++i){
    cv::Mat frame;
    capture >> frame;
    if (i % 8 == 0){
      if (frame.empty()){
        cout << "frame is empty" << endl;
        return -1;
      }
      if (frameArray.size() < 16){
        frameArray.push_back(frame);
      }
      else if (frameArray.size() >= 16){
        frameArray.erase(frameArray.begin());
        frameArray.push_back(frame);
      }
    }
  }
}
```

8.2.2.6 Feature extraction and classification module

In the system flow, the sliding window in the gesture segmentation module requires a sequence of 16 frames of images from the sliding window to be fed into a neural network for classification after each slide. The selected network will output the probability distribution of the sequence over all the gesture categories. So we need to select the category with the highest probability among them as the final recognition result output.

In terms of the choice of feature extraction methods and neural network models, deep neural network based feature extraction tends to perform better due to the fact that it can better adapt to the information in the data itself and does not require the researcher to know a lot about domain related information as manual features do. However, the gestures of interest for the features to be extracted in this project are in videos. Unlike static gestures, dynamic gestures in videos change not change in the spatial dimension but also in the temporal dimension. Therefore it is not enough to model a separate frame of an image in the same way that static gestures are handled. The contextualization of dynamic gestures in the temporal dimension makes it necessary to combine both temporal and spatial information when dealing with the dynamic gesture recognition task.

Therefore we consider using neural networks based on 3D convolutional operations to experiment with the automatic extraction of video gesture features. Compared with the traditional 2D convolution, 3D convolution targets a sequence of video frames. Instead of just dividing the video into a collection of frames and outputting them to multiple images with multiple channels, it applies the convolution kernel to both the time and spatial domains to better integrate the information in the time and spatial domains, which is beneficial for the extraction of the video's features.

As shown in the above figure, 2D convolution is applied to a single-channel image in Fig. 8.11A, and the dimensional information is preserved intact after convolution; Fig. 8.11B indicates that 2D convolution is applied to a multichannel image (multichannel images include 3-color channels of the same picture and multiframe combinations of pictures, i.e., video), and it can be seen that certain dimensional information has been lost after convolution; Fig. 8.11C indicates that 3D convolution is applied to a multichannel image, and the output is still a 3D feature map.

There are various deep neural networks based on 3D convolutional operations, among which C3D [5] and ShuffleNet [6] C3D network obtains feature maps at different scales by successive 3D convolution in the spatiotemporal dimension and uses pooling layers inserted between the convolution layers to downsample the features to obtain more global information. ShuffleNet's idea is to introduce grouped convolution and depth-separable convolutional structures to greatly increase the speed of the network and achieve a better balance between speed and accuracy. We consider the ShuffleNet V2 [7] version, which is more efficient than

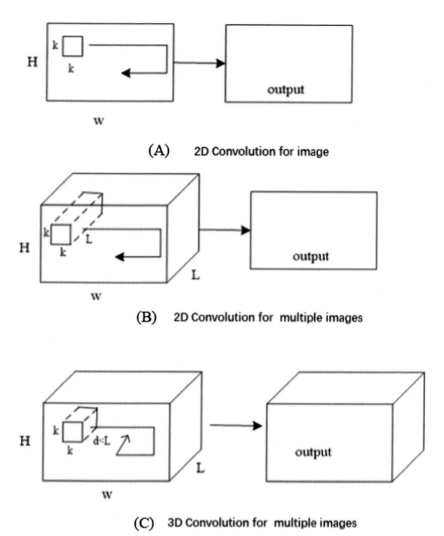

(A)   2D Convolution for image

(B)   2D Convolution for multiple images

(C)   3D Convolution for multiple images

Figure 8.11 Difference between C3D model and traditional CNN model. (A) 2D convolution for images, (B) 2D convolution for multiple images, and (C) 3D convolution for multiple images.

the original ShuffleNet V1. Considering the need for spatiotemporal information modeling, we need to replace the 2D convolution in ShuffleNet V2 with 3D convolution.

To evaluate the performance of both C3D and ShuffleNet V2, we use the accuracy of the two models on the datasets constructed above, both of which were pretrained on the ISO dataset and the Kinect dataset, and the length of the input video was 16 frames. The results are shown in Table 8.1.

The accuracy of the C3D model and ShuffleNet V2 stabilizes at 24 and 100 iterations, respectively. It can be seen that the final classification accuracy of the two models is not much different, and ShuffleNet V2 needs more iterations. However, in terms of model size and computing speed, the model size of ShuffleNet V2 is only about 5% of the C3D model. In terms of model size and speed, the model size of ShuffleNet V2 is only about 5% of that of C3D, and the testing time of ShuffleNet V2 is 70 ms for one sample, while C3D needs 120 ms.

Combining the powerful computing capability provided by the chosen Xavier platform and the high demand for recognition accuracy, we consider the C3D model for this stage of feature extraction and classification. The C3D model supports two different lengths of videos, 16 frames and 32 frames, as inputs. The effect of the two different lengths of inputs on the accuracy has been compared in Fig. 8.12 [8].

The results shown in the figure use the C3D model on the Chalearn LAP IsoGD dataset [9]. The results are obtained after 28 epochs of training on the Chalearn LAP IsoGD dataset. It can be seen that the difference in accuracy between the 16-frame C3D model and the 32-frame C3D model is not significant, regardless of whether RGB data or depth data is used. The 16-frame model has an advantage over the 32-frame model in terms of computing speed. This is the reason why we finally chose the 16-frame C3D model.

Table 8.1 Comparison of the accuracy of C3D model and ShuffleNet V2 model.

Number of model iterations	Classification accuracy
(a) C3D model accuracy	
1	0.8000
11	0.9500
24	0.9500
(b) ShuffleNet V2 model accuracy	
25	0.3000
50	0.8500
100	0.8500

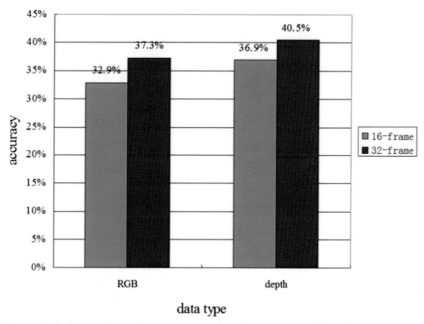

Figure 8.12 Comparison of the accuracy of 16-frame C3D model and 32-frame C3D model.

8.3 Summary

This chapter presents several examples of human—computer interaction based on gesture recognition. The main purpose is to combine some of the gesture recognition techniques described in the previous section with practical applications. It shows the reader how gesture recognition technology can be useful in engineering cases.

References

[1] EternalSmile. (2018, August 23). Gesture recognition will become a major new trend in smart cars. Eeworld. <http://news.eeworld.com.cn/qcdz/2018/ic-news082323591.html>.

[2] A. Arfaoui. Unmanned aerial vehicle: review of onboard sensors, application fields, open problems and research issues. International Journal of Image Processing 11 (1) (2017) 12–24.

[3] Kaipeng Zhang, et al., Joint face detection and alignment using multitask cascaded convolutional networks, IEEE Signal Processing Letters 23 (10) (2016) 1499–1503.

[4] Kaiming He, et al., Deep residual learning for image recognition, Proceedings of the IEEE Conference on Computer Vision and Pattern Recognition (2016).

[5] D. Tran, L. Bourdev, R. Fergus, et al., Learning spatiotemporal features with 3D convolutional networks, Proceedings of the IEEE International Conference on Computer Vision (2015) 4489–4497.

[6] X. Zhang, X. Zhou, M. Lin, et al., Shufflenet: an extremely efficient convolutional neural network for mobile devices, Proceedings of the IEEE Conference on Computer Vision and Pattern Recognition (2018) 6848–6856.

[7] N. Ma, et al., Shufflenet v2: practical guidelines for efficient cnn architecture design, Proceedings of the European Conference on Computer Vision (ECCV (2018).

[8] L. Yunan, et al., Large-scale gesture recognition with a fusion of rgb-d data based on the C3D model, 2016 23rd International Conference on Pattern Recognition (ICPR), IEEE, 2016.

[9] J. Wan, Y. Zhao, S. Zhou, et al., Chalearn looking at people RGB-D isolated and continuous datasets for gesture recognition, Proceedings of the IEEE Conference on Computer Vision and Pattern Recognition Workshops (2016) 56–64.

CHAPTER 9

Exploring development of gesture recognition for future human—computer interaction applications

In the previous chapters, the author has explored various gesture recognition methods and combined them with his own development experience to give an idea of their landing in different application scenarios. This chapter will introduce some specific technical problems faced by gesture recognition algorithms for human—computer interaction and possible solutions to these problems. Based on the current research results of domestic and foreign research institutions, we will further discuss the latest applications and development direction of gesture recognition in human—computer interaction.

9.1 New gesture recognition technology for human—computer interaction

9.1.1 Current issues in gesture recognition technology

As can be seen in the analysis in the previous chapters, with the continuous development of deep learning techniques, gesture recognition methods based on deep neural networks, such as convolutional neural networks, have achieved great improvements in performance. However, it is important to note that most of these techniques are still in the laboratory research stage, despite the breakthroughs they have achieved. Compared with purely dataset-based gesture recognition, gesture recognition in real environments is more open-ended, with more varied changes in environmental factors such as lighting and background. These changing factors can affect the performance of recognition. At the same time, in the real recognition process, gestures do not appear in the form of independent video clips; in most cases, the gesture recognition system will be in a standby state, so a fully functional system in the face

Gesture Recognition
DOI: https://doi.org/10.1016/B978-0-443-28959-0.00009-1

of the user to make noncontrol gestures should not make any response, and when the user begins to give control gestures, it is necessary to accurately give a response. When the user starts to give control gestures, the response needs to be accurate. In addition, compared with most laboratory methods, applications in real environments often have more stringent requirements on real-time performance and hardware cost, so many issues are there that need to be further investigated in the face of human−computer interaction applications in real environments [1], which can be summarized in the following three points.

9.1.1.1 Treatment of irrelevant factors in open environment

As mentioned earlier, a real human−computer interaction environment is in an open environment with a wide variety of backgrounds, lighting, users' clothing, and so on. At the same time, due to the nonspecialized nature of user gestures, different users may have different expressions for the same gesture. It is also important to note that there may also be occlusion of hands and other parts of the body in real environments. Due to the difference in angles, the body parts associated with the gesture may not be fully displayed. These are severe tests for the generalization ability of gesture recognition algorithms.

9.1.1.2 Dynamic gesture tracking and matching

The changing appearance of gestures makes their tracking a challenging research problem. Since the size of the tracking window changes during the tracking process, the problem of tracking drift may occur. At the same time, the gesture of the target gesture changes constantly, which can also lead to a decrease in tracking accuracy. Another important issue is that in the recognition process, facing a large number of constantly appearing noncontrol gestures, the human−computer interaction system needs to make a correct classification to recognize that these actions belong to negative samples rather than a certain class of control gesture actions. In this process, there is a big difference in the number of negative samples and positive samples, and how to balance the proportion of samples and make the correct judgment is also a challenging problem.

9.1.1.3 Algorithmic cost issues

Most of the gesture recognition algorithms are designed with more complex network structures to improve recognition performance, with deeper network hierarchies and a larger number of parameters. Compared with the laboratory environment, where several or even dozens of high-performance graphics cards can be used for model training and testing, the human—computer interaction in real scenarios can't afford such high computational and hardware costs. At the same time, it is worth noting that most of the current algorithms are based on a large number of training samples to ensure the correct rate of recognition, and the labeling of data itself is also a high-cost task. Therefore, how to reduce the number of participants in the model and the model's dependence on large-scale labeled data is also a problem that must be considered in the process of applying gesture recognition algorithms to the ground.

9.1.2 Directions for future research

Based on the above issues, possible future research directions for gesture recognition are explored here from the perspectives of 3D gesture reconstruction, gesture tracking, model compression, and semisupervised learning.

9.1.2.1 3D gesture reconstruction based on multisensor devices

In Chapter 6, we explored methods for gesture recognition based on multimodal data. However, these different modal data are still essentially visual data, and despite their complementarity, they essentially treat gestures as 2D structures, which makes it difficult to solve the problem of appearance change and gesture rotation of the gesture model. At the same time, both the infrared camera and the RGB-D camera represented by Kinect have greater requirements for the background of the gesture demonstration. When there are other objects in the background or other heat sources, it will interfere with the accuracy of gesture recognition. In real-world scenarios, this type of complex background problem is unavoidable. Therefore a feasible idea is to get away from the limitations of 2D vision and utilize devices such as millimeter-wave radar to construct a 3D stereoscopic visual space to solve problems such as gesture occlusion that may exist in a single-view background.

9.1.2.2 Gesture feature learning based on multiscale representation

In general, the proportion of gestures in the whole image is small, so when learning gesture features, the overall features and local features of gestures should be fully considered. It is necessary to model the macroscopic information, such as the position of the whole gesture in space, through the overall features, and it is also necessary to characterize the details of the gesture based on different scales and to learn various detailed information about the gesture. In this way, the joint representation of target gestures of different sizes is realized, which in turn improves the expressive ability of gesture features.

9.1.2.3 Model compression based on network structure search

As mentioned in the previous section, gesture recognition applications in real-world scenarios tend to be more demanding in terms of the number of parameters and hardware devices. Therefore compression of the model to reduce the number of parameters so that it can be run on mobile devices with less computational power is also a problem that needs to be investigated. Neural architecture search (NAS) is a technique that has emerged in recent years. Compared with the previous method of network optimization by manually setting hyperparameters, the NAS-based method can automatically optimize the parameters to obtain the best network structure, reduce unnecessary parameters in the network, and thus improve the performance of the network. In addition, model pruning is also an important technique. It is widely recognized that although more complex network structures are needed to achieve better results, such models generally have a high degree of redundancy, and many feature maps have a weak response. Therefore the model can be pruned to reduce the association between the model and the low-response features, that is, it can reduce the consumption of time and space resources required for the model to run while reducing the accuracy, or even possibly increasing the accuracy.

9.1.2.4 Semisupervised modeling for massive open data

Not only in the field of gesture recognition, existing supervised learning methods mostly rely on accurate labeling, but the data labeling itself is a very consuming work in terms of human and material costs, especially with the development of the Internet, the amount of data has seen explosive growth. Therefore to address the problem of the difficulty of labeling massive video data, it is necessary to construct semisupervised models for video classification and action recognition that can effectively utilize a large amount of unlabeled data without labeling by generalizing and iterating the model learned on a small amount of labeled data over the unlabeled data to improve the generalization ability of the model to better deal with the problem of gesture recognition in open environments.

9.2 New applications of gesture recognition in human—computer interaction

9.2.1 Intelligent driving

It is well known that there are certain unsafe factors for automobile drivers to interact with automobile control devices while driving, mainly because drivers may be distracted from driving during human—computer interaction with automobiles. Currently, in-vehicle human—computer interaction is mainly carried out through touch display screens and voice. Although the touch precision and response speed of the touch display have been continuously improved, the fact that touch control must rely on the user's contact with the screen surface limits the user's operating space and flexibility. In terms of voice recognition, although the related technologies and products are more mature, voice recognition still has limitations in handling persistent commands, such as adjusting the volume of the stereo and the progress of the music [2]. The flexibility of gesture recognition can better complement the above two technologies. At present, automobile manufacturers represented by BMW, Jaguar, and Mercedes-Benz have already added gesture recognition technology to their automobile control systems. For example, Fig. 9.1 shows that users can answer calls, reject calls, adjust the volume and other operations through gestures, or click, move, zoom, and other commonly used controls on the car screen. This multilevel interaction mode, which integrates touch, voice, and gesture control, is gradually being noticed by automobile manufacturers.

9.2.2 Smart home

Smart home control systems are known by many names, including smart home, home automation, and integrated home systems. Of these names, smart home is the most familiar. The system generally uses the home as a platform to integrate technologies such as integrated wiring, network communications, security, and automation. The goal is to easily control home electronics, including audio, video, home office, telecommunications, security, lighting, air conditioning, and more. As shown in Fig. 9.2, taking TV as an example, in a smart home environment, people can more conveniently perform control functions such as volume adjustment and channel switching through gestures and voice.

Smart homes offer greater security and convenience. These systems provide peace of mind by alerting residents to emergencies regardless of

Figure 9.1 Schematic of the application of gesture recognition in smart driving.

Figure 9.2 Schematic of application of gesture recognition in smart home.

their location, whether at work or on vacation. By intelligently managing household devices, smart home systems optimize energy consumption, transitioning appliances to sleep mode when idle and ensuring efficient energy use when active. Furthermore, for elderly individuals living alone and people with mobility impairments, smart homes offer critical real-time health monitoring and timely medical alerts in case of emergencies, thereby providing an added layer of safety and support.

In a smart home, human—computer interaction is an important part. Compared with the traditional human—computer interaction mode, the contactless human—computer interaction realized by using gesture recognition is more flexible and natural. It allows users to control various smart home appliances anywhere in the home using only gesture movements. For example, instead of using a remote control, a user can switch on or off the lights in a room, adjust the volume of a TV, or adjust the temperature of a refrigerator with a simple customized gesture. This is undoubtedly an important development direction for smart homes, and many designers are trying to design products accordingly. In 2016 French designer Vivien Muller designed a remote control called Bearbot [3]. The remote control can be paired with various remote controls at home through an app, and then by recording various gesture commands, users can control various home appliances by gestures alone. Similarly, Israel's Eyesight has launched a tool called Onecue, which allows users to control home appliances with gestures and their arms, replacing the plethora of remotes available at home [4]. Onecue's controls are uncomplicated, with a small display on the front, on which icons represent the appliances they are currently controlling. Onecue is not complicated to control;, it has a small display on the front with icons representing the appliances it is controlling, and the user can switch between them and control the functions of the current appliance with a simple wave of the hand.

9.2.3 Drone control

A drone is a vehicle that is controlled by an on-board flight computer or a handheld remote control device. While the development of UAVs was first driven by military applications, in recent years, a variety of technological advances have led to the development of a low-cost civilian solution for nonmilitary applications. We are seeing an increasing number of small UAVs designed for use in livelihood areas such as photogrammetry, remote sensing, forestry and agriculture, environment, and energy [5].

Conventional UAV control is generally carried out via a remote control, where the user sends operational commands to the UAV via joysticks and buttons on the remote control. This traditional control method can communicate with the drone over long distances and can be adapted to a wide range of flight tasks in different environments. However, the disadvantage is that it is more demanding for the operator, who needs to learn a series of complicated usage methods and operation commands. With the development of gesture recognition technology, combining gesture recognition with UAV control has undoubtedly become a new mode of UAV control. As shown in Fig. 9.3, by using gesture recognition technology, users do not need to learn professional operation instructions and can control the flight of the UAV only through user-defined gesture movements. This new model of drone control is more capable of meeting the needs of the general public for drone use. DJI Drones, a well-known domestic drone manufacturer, has already carried gesture recognition technology on its drone products. Their Spark Xiao drone launched in 2017 can be operated with gestures without the need for a remote control to operate the drone. Users only need to perform simple gestures to realize the drone's position adjustment, flight direction control, selfie, recall, palm landing, and other functions. After that, DJI also launched its successor products equipped with gesture recognition technology, such as Mavic Air and Mavic 2 [6]. As research continues to advance, gesture recognition and drone control will be more closely integrated. The Shenyang Institute

Figure 9.3 Example of gesture recognition applied to UAV control.

of Automation (SIAM) of the Chinese Academy of Sciences has also launched a human—machine collaborative intelligent drone system [7], which combines vision-based intelligent gesture recognition technology with a drone flight platform to realize the control of the drone's mission through human gestures. According to He Yuqing, a researcher at the SIAM, China Academy, this system has realized the first human—machine interaction flight experiment under outdoor strong light interference in China, greatly improving the system's adaptability to real outdoor environments and shortening the distance between future intelligent drones and people's real lives. In the future, people will be able to control the drone with a few simple gestures.

9.2.4 Robot control

With the development of robotics technology, robots have gradually entered people's daily life from the laboratory. Robots have been able to replace human beings in factories to do part of the work and also in daily life to provide people with entertainment and help. As of 2020, world wide 2.6 million industrial robots have been put into use, and interactions between humans and robots are becoming more frequent. Therefore the design and development of human friendly and adaptable robots play a pivotal role in today's manufacturing industry. As shown in Fig. 9.4, hand gestures, as a common way of communication between people, contain

Figure 9.4 Schematic of robot interaction using gestures.

more information and have the advantages of being natural, simple, and direct. Therefore, robot control based on gesture recognition technology is easier and friendlier, and its importance is becoming more and more prominent.

It is because gesture recognition has an important role in the field of noncontact robot control that in recent years research teams at home and abroad have proposed many ways to control robots using gestures. MIT's Computer Science and Artificial Intelligence Laboratory has developed a system [8] that can control a robot by relying on brain waves and hand gestures. While the system acquires gestures through wearable devices, it also collects brainwaves from a person's movements to provide the robot with the appropriate brainwave patterns to provide assistance, for example, to the elderly, speech- or mobility-impaired people, etc. Zhongxing Duan and Bai Yang [9], on the other hand, utilized convolutional neural networks for gesture learning and designed a gesture-guided robot demonstration system using a robot operating system to control the robot in the modes of learning, coding, and execution.

9.3 Summary

This chapter analyzes several problems faced by gesture recognition in the current human—computer interaction application environment and possible research directions to solve these problems. It also introduces new applications of gesture recognition in human—computer interaction in combination with the research results of domestic and foreign research organizations.

References

[1] Q. Tian, H. Yang, Q. Liang, et al., A review of visual dynamic gesture recognition, Journal of Zhejiang University of Technology (Natural Science Edition) 43 (4) (2020) 557—569.
[2] Eeworld. Gesture recognition will become a major new trend in smart cars [EB/OL]. <http://news.eeworld.com.cn/qcdz/2018/ic-news082323591.html>, 2018.
[3] Pinnacle Technology, Gesture can control all appliances at home, Bearbot is simply handsome! [EB/OL]. <https://www.sohu.com/a/114158964_364422>, 2016.
[4] ifanr, Onecue gestures to play with appliances [EB/OL]. <https://www.ifanr.com/news/471926>, 2014.
[5] A. Arfaoui, Unmanned aerial vehicle: review of onboard sensors, application fields, open problems and research issues, International Journal of Image Processing 11 (1) (2017) 12—24.

[6] Mai Weiqi, DJI Mavic air released, with 7 cameras you can really do whatever you want [EB/OL]. <https://www.sohu.com/a/218608156_602994>, 2018.

[7] W. Ying, Three robots of Shenyang Institute of Automation, Chinese Academy of Sciences, debut [EB/OL]. <http://www.cas.cn/cm/201705/t20170522_4602213.shtml>, 2017.

[8] A. Simons, How to control robots with brainwaves and hand gestures [EB/OL]. <https://news.mit.edu/2018/how-to-control-robots-with-brainwaves-hand-gestures-mit-csail-0620>, 2018.

[9] Z. Duan, Y. Bai., Design of robot demonstration and teaching system combined with deep learning, Computerized Measurement and Control 28 (11) (2020) 164−169.

Index

Note: Page numbers followed by "*f*" and "*t*" refer to figures and tables, respectively.